HEAVEN
Awaits

D. L. MOODY

WHITAKER
HOUSE

Publisher's Note: This new edition from Whitaker House has been updated for the modern reader. Words, expressions, and sentence structure have been revised for clarity and readability.

All Scripture quotations are taken from the King James Version (KJV) of the Holy Bible.

HEAVEN AWAITS

(Previously published as *Heaven: How to Get There*)

ISBN-13: 978-1-60374-036-4
ISBN-10: 1-60374-036-8
Printed in the United States of America
© 1982 by Whitaker House

Whitaker House
1030 Hunt Valley Circle
New Kensington, PA 15068
www.whitakerhouse.com

2 3 4 5 6 7 8 9 10 ⊔⊔ 15 14 13 12 11 10 09 08

CONTENTS

Chapter 1

HEAVEN...ITS HOPE

That unchangeable home is for you and me,
Where Jesus of Nazareth stands;
The King of all kingdoms forever is He,
And He holdeth out crowns in His hands.

Oh, how sweet it will be in that beautiful land,
So free from all sorrow and pain;
With songs on our lips and with harps in our hands,
To meet one another again.

HEAVEN...ITS HOPE

Many people believe that anything said about heaven is mere speculation. They talk about heaven like the air. Now there would not be so much in Scripture on this subject if God had wanted to leave the human race in the darkness about it. All Scripture, we are told, is given by inspiration from God. It is beneficial when used for doctrine, reproof, correction, and instruction in righteousness, so that the man of God may be perfect—thoroughly furnished with all good works. What the Bible says about heaven is just as true as what it says about everything else. It is inspired. What we are taught about heaven could not have come to us in any other way except by inspiration. No one knew anything about it but God, and so if we want to find out anything about it, we have to turn to His Word.

Dr. Hodge, a professor at Princeton Theological Seminary, said that the best evidence of the Bible being the Word of God is to be found between its own two covers. It proves itself. In this respect, it is like Christ, whose character proclaimed the divinity of His person. Christ showed Himself to be more than a man by what He did. The Bible shows itself to be more than a human book by what it says. It is not, however, because the Bible is *written* with more than human skill—far surpassing Shakespeare or any other human author—or that its knowledge of character and the eloquence it contains are beyond the powers of man, that we believe it to be inspired.

Men's ideas differ about the extent to which human skill can go, but the reason why we believe the Bible is inspired is so simple that the humblest child of God can comprehend it. If the proof of its divine origin lay in its wisdom alone, a simple and uneducated man might not be able to believe it. We believe it is inspired because there is nothing in it that could *not* have come from God. God is wise, and God is good. There is nothing in the Bible that is not wise, and there is nothing in it that is not good. If the

Bible had anything in it that was opposed to reason, or to our sense of right, then we might think that it was like all the books in the world that are written merely by men.

Books that are just human books, like merely human lives, contain a great deal of foolishness and a great deal that is wrong. The life of Christ alone was perfect, being both human and divine. None of the other religious volumes, like the Koran, that claim a divine origin, agree with common sense. There is nothing at all in the Bible that does not conform to common sense. What it tells us about the world having been destroyed by a flood, and Noah and his family alone being saved, is no more incredible than what is being taught in the schools—that all of the earth we now see, and everything on it, came out of a ball of fire. It is a great deal easier to believe that man was created in the image of God than it is to believe as some young men and women are being taught now—that he was once a monkey.

Like all the other wonderful works of God, this book bears the sure stamp of its author.

It is like Him. Though man plants the seeds, God makes the flowers. They are perfect and beautiful like Himself. Men wrote what is in the Bible, but the work is God's. As a rule, the more refined people are, the fonder they are of the flowers; and, as a rule, the better they are, the more they love the Bible. The fondness for flowers refines people, and the love of the Bible makes them better. All that is in the Bible about God, man, redemption, and a future state agrees with our own ideas of right, with our reasonable fears, and with our personal experiences. All historical things are told in the manner in which the world thought about them at the time they were written. What the Bible says about heaven is not half as strange as what Professor Proctor, the English astronomer, said about the hosts of stars that are beyond the range of any telescope. Yet, people very often think that science is all fact and that religion is only fancy. A great many people think that Jupiter and many more of the stars around us are inhabited. Yet they cannot bring themselves to believe that there is a life beyond this earth for immortal souls. The true Christian puts faith before reason and believes that reason always goes wrong when faith is set aside. If people would only read their Bibles more, and study what there is to be found there about heaven, then they would not be as worldly minded as they are. They would not have their hearts set on things down here, but would seek the imperishable things above.

Earth, the Home of Sin

It seems perfectly reasonable that God should have given us a glimpse of the future, for we will eventually lose some of our friends by death. Then, the first thought that comes to us is, "Where have they gone?" When a loved one is taken away from us, how often we think that very thing! How we wonder if we will ever see them again, and where and when it will be! Then, we turn to this blessed Book, for there is no other book in all the world that can give us the slightest comfort. There is no other book that can tell us where our loved ones have gone.

Not long ago, I met an old friend. As I took him by the hand and asked about his family, tears came trickling down his cheeks, and he said:

"I haven't any now."

"What," I said, "is your wife dead?"

"Yes, sir."

"And all your children, too?"

"Yes, all gone," he said, "and I am left here, desolate and alone."

Would anyone deprive that man of the hope that he will meet his dear ones again? Would anyone persuade him that there is not a future where the lost will be found? No, we need not forget our dear loved ones. But, we may forever cling to the enduring hope that there will be a time when we can meet again and be blessed in that land of everlasting suns. Heaven is where the soul drinks from the living streams of love that roll past God's high throne.

There are none who don't question the future in their innermost hearts. There are men who say that there is no heaven. I was once talking with a man who said he thought there was nothing to justify us in believing

13

in any other heaven than we know here on earth. If this is heaven, it is a very strange one—this world of sickness, sorrow, and sin. From the depths of my heart, I pity the man or woman who has that idea.

This world that so many think is heaven is the home of sin, a hospital of sorrow, a place with nothing in it to satisfy the soul. Men travel all over it and then want to get out of it. The more one sees of the world, the less he thinks of it. People soon grow tired of the best pleasures it has to offer. Someone has said that the world is a stormy sea whose every wave is filled with the wrecks of mortals who perish in it. Every time we breathe, someone is dying. We all know that we are going to stay here a very short while. Our life is only a vapor. It is just a mere shadow.

We meet one another, as someone has said, salute one another, pass on, and are gone. Another has said that it is just an inch of time, and then eternal ages roll on. It seems to me that it is perfectly reasonable for us to want to read on, to find out where we are going, and where our friends are who have gone on before us. The longest time man has to live has no more proportion to eternity than a drop of dew has to the ocean.

Cities of the Past

Look at the cities of the past. There is Babylon. It was founded by a woman named Semiramis. She had two million men at work for years building it. It is nothing but dust now. Nearly a thousand years ago, some historian wrote that the ruins of Nebuchadnezzar's palace were still standing, but men were afraid to go near them because they were full of scorpions and snakes. That's the sort of ruin that greatness often comes to in our own day.

Nineveh is gone. Its towers and fortresses have fallen. The traveler who tries to see Carthage can't see much of it. Corinth, once the seat of luxury and art, is only a shapeless mass now. Ephesus, long the metropolis of Asia, the Paris of that day, was crowded with buildings as large as the capitol at Washington. I am told it looks more like a neglected graveyard now than anything else. Granada is now the home of lions and jackals. It was once very grand, with its twelve gates and towers. The Alhambra, the palace of the Mohammedan kings, was situated there. Animals probably play with the monarchs' bones now. Little pieces of the once grand and beautiful cities of Herculanaeum and Pompeii are now being sold in the shops for relics.

Jerusalem, once one of the grandest cities of the universe, is but a shadow of itself. Thebes—for thousands of years, almost until the coming of Christ, the largest and wealthiest city of the world—is now a mass of decay. Very little of Athens and other proud cities of olden times remain to tell the story of their downfall. God drives His plowshare through cities, and they are upheaved like furrows in the field. "*Behold*," says Isaiah 40:15, 17,

> *The nations are as a drop of a bucket, and are counted as the small dust of the balance; behold, he taketh up the isles as very little things... All nations*

> *before him are as nothing; and they are counted to him less than nothing, and vanity.*

See how Antioch has fallen! When Paul preached there, it was a superb metropolis. A wide street, over three miles long, stretching across the entire city, was ornamented with rows of columns and covered galleries. At, every corner, carved statues stood to commemorate their great men, whose names we have never even heard. These people are never heard of now. But the poor preaching tentmaker, the apostle Paul, stands out as one of the grandest characters in all history. In Antioch, the finest specimens of Grecian art decorated the shrines of the temples, and the baths and the aqueducts were such as are never approached in elegance now. Men then, as now, were seeking honors, wealth, and mighty names. They were seeking to enshrine their names and records in perishable clay. We are told that mountains over seven hundred feet high were enclosed within the walls. Rocky precipices and deep ravines gave a wild and picturesque

17

character to the city of which no modern city gives us an example. These heights were fortified in a marvelous manner, which gave them strange and startling effects. The vast population of this brilliant city, combining all the art and cultivation of Greece with the levity, the luxury, and the superstition of Asia, was as intent on pleasure as the population of any of our great cities are today. They had their shows, their games, their races and dances, their sorcerers, puzzles, buffoons, and "miracle-workers," and the whole population constantly sought something to stimulate and gratify the most corrupt desires of the soul.

This is pretty much what we find the masses of the people in our great cities doing now. Antioch was even worse than Athens, for the so-called worship they indulged in was not only idolatrous, but was a mixture of the grossest passions to which man descends. It was here that Paul came to preach the glad tidings of the gospel of Christ. It was here that his converts were first called Christians. Previously, all followers of Christ had been called "saints" or "brethren." As has been well said, out of that spring at Antioch a mighty stream has flowed to water the world. These are no more: Astarte, "the queen of heaven," whom they worshipped, Diana, Apollo, the Pharisee and Sadducee; but the "despised" Christians yet live. That heathen city, which would not take Christianity to its heart and keep it, fell. Cities that do not have the refining and restraining influences of Christianity well established in them seldom amount to much in the long run. They grow dim in the light of ages. Few of our great cities in this country are a hundred years old as yet. For nearly a thousand years, Antioch prospered; yet it fell.

Going to Emigrate

I do not think that it is wrong for us to think and talk about heaven. I like to locate heaven and find out all I can about it. I expect to live there through all eternity. If I was going to dwell in any place in this country—if I was going to make it my home—I would want to inquire about the place, its climate, the neighbors I would have, and everything that I could learn about it. If any of you were going to emigrate, that would be the way you would feel. Well, we are all going to emigrate in a very little while to a country that is very far away. We are going to spend eternity in another world—a grand and glorious world where God reigns. Is it not natural, then, that we should look, listen, and try to find out who is already there and how to get there?

Soon after I was converted, a non-believer asked me why I looked up when I prayed. He said that heaven was no more above us than below us—that heaven was everywhere. Well, I was greatly bewildered, and the next time I prayed it seemed almost as if I was praying into the air. Since then, I have become better acquainted with the Bible, and I have come to see that heaven *is* above us. It is upward, and not downward. The Spirit of God is everywhere, but God is in heaven, and heaven is above our heads. It does not matter what part of the globe we may stand on, heaven is above us.

In Genesis 17 it says that God went *up* from Abraham; and in John 3 that He came *down* from heaven. Also, in Acts 1 we find that Christ went *up* (not down), and a cloud received Him out of sight. Thus, we see heaven is up. The very arrangement of the atmosphere about the earth declares the seat of God's glory to be above us. Job 3:4 says, *"Let not God regard it from **above"*** (emphasis added), and we find the psalmist declaring, *"The Lord is **high** above all nations, and his glory **above** the heavens"* (Psalm 113:4, emphasis added).

Again in Deuteronomy we find, *"Who shall go up for us to heaven?"* (Deuteronomy 30:12). Thus, all through Scripture we find that the location of heaven is upward and beyond the sky. This universe, with its many bright worlds scattered throughout, is so vast that heaven must be an extensive realm. Yet this need not surprise us. It is not for shortsighted man to inquire why God made heaven so extensive that the lights along the way can be seen from any part or side of this little world.

In the prophecy of Jeremiah we are told:

He hath made the earth by his power;
he hath established the world by his
wisdom, and hath stretched out the
heaven by his understanding.

(Jeremiah 51:15)

Yet how little we really know of that power, wisdom, or understanding! As it says in Job 26:14, *"Lo, these are parts of his ways: but how little a portion is heard of him? but the thunder of his power who can understand?"* This is the Word of God. As we find in Isaiah 42:5:

Thus saith God the Lord, he that cre-
ated the heavens, and stretched them
out; he that spread forth on the earth,
and that which cometh out of it; he that
giveth breath unto the people upon it,
and spirit to them that walk therein.

The discernment of God's power—the messages of heaven—do not always come in great things. We read in 1 Kings 19:11–12:

And, behold, the Lord passed by, and a
great and strong wind rent the moun-
tains, and brake in pieces the rocks

*before the Lord; but the Lord was not
in the wind: and after the wind an
earthquake; but the Lord was not in
the earthquake: and after the earthquake a fire; but the Lord was not in
the fire: and after the fire a still small
voice.*

God speaks to His children in a still,
small voice. Some people are trying to find
out just how far away heaven is. There is one
thing we know about it—that God can hear
us when we pray. I do not believe there has
ever been a tear shed for sin since Adam's
fall in Eden to the present time that God has
not witnessed. He is not too far from this
earth for us to go to Him. If there is a sigh
that comes from a burdened heart today,
God will hear it. If there is a cry coming up
from a heart broken on account of sin, God
will hear it. He is not so far away—heaven
is not so far away as to be inaccessible to the
smallest child. In 2 Chronicles 7:14 we read:

*If my people, which are called by my
name, shall humble themselves, and
pray, and seek my face, and turn from*

*their wicked ways, then will I hear
from heaven, and will forgive their
sins, and will heal their land.*

When I was in Dublin, they were telling
me about a father who had lost a little boy,
and he had not thought about the future
because he had been so entirely taken up
with this world and its affairs. But when that
little boy, his only child, died, the father's
heart was broken. Every night when he got
home from work they would find him with
his tallow candle and his Bible in his room.
He was hunting up all that he could find
in Scripture about heaven. When someone
asked him what he was doing, he said he was
trying to find out where his child had gone.
I think he was a reasonable man. I suppose
there is not a man or woman who does not
have dear ones who are gone. Will we close
this book today, or will we read it to try to
find out where our loved ones are?

I was reading, some time ago, an account
of a father—a minister—who had lost a
child. He had gone to a great many funer-
als, offering comfort to others in sorrow. But

now the iron had entered his own soul, and a brother minister had come to officiate and preach the funeral sermon. After this minister got through speaking, the father got up, stood right at the head of the coffin, and looked at the face of that loved child who was gone. He said that a few years before, when he had first come into that parish, he used to look over the river. He took no interest in the people over there because they were all strangers to him, and none of them belonged to his parish. But, he said, a few years ago a young man came into his home, married his daughter, and she went over the river to live. When his child went over there, he suddenly became interested in the inhabitants, and every morning as he would get up he would look out of the window and look over there at her home. But now, he said, another child has left home. "She has gone over a different river, and heaven seems dearer and nearer to me than it ever has before."

My friends, let us believe the Word of God, that heaven is not a myth. And let us be prepared to follow the dear ones who have gone before us. There, and there alone, can we find the peace we seek.

Seeking a Better Country

What has been, and is now, one of the strongest feelings in the human heart? Is it not to find some better place, some lovelier spot, than we have now? Men everywhere are seeking this, and they can have it, if they truly want it. But instead of looking down, they must look up to find it. As men grow in knowledge, they compete with each other more and more to make their homes attractive. But the brightest home on earth is only an empty barn compared to the mansions that are in the skies.

What do we look for at the decline and close of life? Is it not some sheltered place, some quiet spot, where, if we cannot have constant rest, we may at least have a foretaste of what it is to be? What was it that led Columbus, not knowing what his fate would be, across the unsailed western seas, if it was not the hope of finding a better country? It was this that sustained the hearts of the Pilgrim fathers, driven from their native land by persecution, as they faced an iron-bound, savage coast, with an unexplored territory beyond. They were cheered and upheld by the hope of reaching a free and fruitful country where they could be at rest and worship God in peace.

The Christian's hope of heaven is somewhat similar, only it is not an undiscovered country and cannot be compared with anything we know on earth. Perhaps nothing but our shortsightedness keeps us from seeing the celestial gates open to us, and nothing but the deafness of our ears prevents us from hearing the joyful ringing of the bells of heaven. There are constant sounds around us that we cannot hear, and the sky is studded with bright worlds that our eyes have never seen. Little as we know about this bright and radiant land, glimpses of its beauty come to us now and then.

It is said by travelers that in climbing the Alps, the houses of distant villages can be seen with great distinctness, so that sometimes the number of panes of glass in a church window can be counted. The distance looks so short that the place seems almost at hand, but after hours and hours of climbing, it does not look any closer. This is because of the clearness of the atmosphere. By perseverance, however, the place is reached at last, and the tired traveler finds rest. So sometimes when we dwell in high altitudes of grace, heaven seems very near, and the hills of Beulah are in full view. At other times, the clouds and fogs that come through suffering and sin cut off our sight. We are just as near heaven in the one case as we are in the other, and we are just as sure of gaining it if we only remain in the path of Christ.

I have read that on the shores of the Adriatic sea, the wives of fishermen whose husbands are far out at sea are in the habit of going down to the seashore at night and sweetly singing the first verse of some beautiful hymn. After they have sung it, they listen until they hear, brought on the wind, across the sea, the second verse sung by their brave husbands as they are tossed by the gale—and both are happy. Perhaps, if we would listen, we too might hear on this sea-tossed world of ours some sound, some whisper, borne from afar to tell us there is a heaven which is our home. When we sing out hymns on the shores of earth, perhaps we may hear their sweet echoes breaking in music on the sands of time, and cheering the hearts of those who are pilgrims and strangers along the way. Yes, we need to look up—out, beyond this low earth—and build higher in our thoughts and actions, even here!

You know, when a man is going up in a balloon, he takes in sand as a ballast to control his altitude. When he wants to climb a little higher, he throws out a little of the ballast, and then he will mount a little higher. He throws out a little more ballast, and he mounts still higher. The more he throws out, the higher he gets. So, the nearer we get to God, the more things of this world we have to throw out. Let go of them. Do not let us set our hearts and affections on them, but do what the Master tells us—lay up for ourselves treasures in heaven.

In England, I was told of a lady who had been bedridden for years. She was one of those saints whom God polishes up for the kingdom—for I believe that there are a good many saints in this world whom we never hear about. We never see their names heralded through the press. They live very near the Master, very near heaven.

Now, it was one of those saints, a lady, who said that for a long time she used to take great pleasure in watching a bird that came to make its nest near her window. One year it came to make its nest, and it began to make it so low she was afraid something would happen to the young. Every day that she saw that bird busy at work making its nest, she kept saying, "O bird, build higher!" She could see that the bird was going to come to grief and disappointment. At last, the bird got its nest done, laid its eggs, and hatched its young. Every morning the lady looked out to see if the nest was still there, and she saw the old bird bringing food for the little ones. She took a great deal of pleasure in looking at it. But one morning she woke up, looked out, and saw nothing but feathers scattered all around. She said,

"Ah, the cat has got the old bird and all its young." It would have been a mercy to have torn that nest down. That is what God does for us very often—just snatches things away before it is too late. Now, I think that is what we want to say to church people—that if you build on earth you will be disappointed. God is telling us to build up yonder. It is a good deal better to have life in Christ and God than anywhere else. I would rather have my life hid with Christ in God than be in Eden as Adam was. Adam might have remained in Paradise for 16,000 years and then fallen, but if ours is hid in Christ, how safe!

Chapter 2

HEAVEN...ITS INHABITANTS

A little way! I know it is not far
To that clear home where my beloved are;
And still my heart sits, like a bird, upon
The empty nest, and mourns its treasures gone,
Plumed for their flight, And vanished quite
Ah me! where is the comfort? though I say
They have, but journeyed on a little way.

The inhabitants of heaven will be select. No one who studies Scripture can doubt that. There are a good many kinds of aristocracy in this world, but the aristocracy of heaven will be the aristocracy of holiness. The humblest sinner on earth will be an aristocrat there. It says in Isaiah 57:15:

> *For thus saith the high and lofty One that inhabiteth eternity, whose name is Holy; I will dwell in the high and holy place, with him that is of a contrite and humble spirit.*

Now what could be plainer than that? No one who is not of a contrite and humble spirit will dwell with God in His high and holy place.

If there is anything that ought to make heaven near to Christians, it is knowing that God and all their loved ones will be there. What is it that makes home so attractive?

Is it because we have a beautiful house? Is it because we have beautiful lawns? Is it because we have beautiful trees around that home? Is it because we have beautiful paintings on the walls inside? Is it because we have beautiful furniture? Is that all that makes home so attractive and so beautiful? No, it is the loved ones in it; it is the loved ones there.

I remember after being away from home for some time, I went back to see my honored mother, and I thought in going back I would take her by surprise. I thought that I would steal in unexpectedly. But when I found she had gone away, the old place didn't seem like home at all. I went into one room, then another, and I went all through the house, but I could not find that loved mother. I said to some member of the family, "Where is Mother?" and they said she had gone out for awhile. Well, home had lost its charm to me; it was that mother who made home so sweet to me, and it is the loved ones that make home so sweet to everyone. It is the loved ones that are going to make heaven so sweet to all of us. Christ is there; God the Father is there. And, many, many who were dear to us, who lived on earth, are there—and we will be with them eventually.

We find clearly in Matthew 18:10 that the angels are there:

Take heed that ye despise not one of these little ones; for I say unto you, That in heaven their angels do always behold the face of my Father which is in heaven.

Their angels always behold the Father's face! We will have good company up there—not only those who have been redeemed, but those who have never been lost—the angels. Those who have never known what it is to transgress, those who have never known what it is to be disobedient, and those who have obeyed Him from the very morning of creation will be there. It says in Luke that when Gabriel came down to tell Zachariah that he was to be the father of the forerunner of Jesus Christ, Zachariah doubted him. Gabriel had never been doubted before, and that doubt is met with the declaration: "*I am*

Gabriel, that stand in the presence of God" (Luke 1:19). What a glorious thing to be able to say!

It has been said that there will be three things that will surprise us when we get to heaven: one, to find many there whom we did not expect to find there; another, to find some not there whom we had expected; a third, and perhaps the greatest wonder, will be to find ourselves there.

A poor woman once told Rowland Hill, the famous British soldier, that the way to heaven was short, easy, and simple, comprising only three steps: out of self, into Christ, and then into glory. We have a shorter way now—out of self and into Christ—and we are there. As a dead man cannot inherit an estate, no more can a dead soul inherit heaven. The soul must be resurrected in Christ. Among the good whom we hope to meet in heaven, we are told there will be every variety of character, taste, and disposition. There is not one mansion there, but many. There is not one gate into heaven, but many. There are not only gates on the north, but three gates on the east, three gates on the west, and three gates on the south.

From opposite quarters of the theological compass, the religious world, human life and character, through different expressions of their common faith and hope, different modes of conversion, and different portions of the Holy Scripture, the weary travelers will enter the heavenly city, and meet each other—not without surprise—on the shores of the same river of life. And on those shores, they will find a tree bearing not the same kind of fruit always and at all times, but *"twelve manner of fruits"* (Revelation 22:2). There is a different fruit for every different turn of mind: for the patient suffer, the active servant, the holy and humble philosopher, the spirits of just men now at last made perfect. And, *"the leaves of the tree shall be for the healing,"* not of one single church or people only, not for the Scotchman or the Englishman only, but for the *"healing of the nations"* (verse 2). It is for the Frenchman, the German, the Italian, the Russian—for all those from whom its fruits have been farthest removed, but who, nevertheless, have *"hungered and thirsted after righteousness,"* and who therefore *"shall be filled"* (Matthew 5:6).

A famous theologian, who was advanced in years, said, "When I was a boy, I thought of heaven as a great, shining city, with vast walls and domes and spires, and with nobody in it except white-robed angels, who were strangers to me. By and by, my little brother died and I thought of a great city with walls and domes and spires, and a flock of cold, unknown angels, and one little fellow that I was acquainted with. He was the only one I knew at that time. Then another brother died, and there were two that I knew. As I grew older, my acquaintances began to die, and the flock continually grew; but it was not till I had sent one of my own children to his heavenly Parent [God] that I began to think I had gone a little of the way in myself. A second went, a third went, a fourth went, and by that time I had so many acquaintances in heaven that I did not see any more walls and domes and spires. I began to think of the residents of the celestial city. And now so many of my acquaintances have gone there, that it sometimes seems to me that I know more in heaven than I do on earth."

We Will Live Forever

It says in John 12:26, *"If any man serve me, let him follow me; and where I am, there shall also my servant be."* I cannot agree with people who say that Paul has been sleeping in the grave, and is still there, after the storms of 1,900 years. I cannot believe that he who loved the Master, who had such a burning zeal for Him, has been separated from Him in an unconscious state. This is Christ's prayer:

> *Father, I will that they also, whom thou hast given me, be with me where I am; that they may behold my glory, which thou, hast given me.*
>
> (John 17:24)

Now, when a man believes on the Lord Jesus Christ, he receives eternal life. A great many people make a mistake right there: "He that believeth on the Son hath— h-a-t-h—hath everlasting life" (John 3:36).

It does not say he will have it when he dies. It is in the present tense. It is mine now—if I believe. He is the gift of God, and that is enough. You can't bury the gift of God; you can't bury eternal life. All the grave diggers in the world can't dig a grave large enough or deep enough to hold eternal life. All the coffin makers of the world can't make a coffin large enough and deep enough to hold eternal life. That is mine; it is mine!

I believe that when Paul said, "*To be absent from the body, and to be present with the Lord*" (2 Corinthians 5:8), he meant what he said. He meant that he was not going to be separated from Him for 1,900 years. The Spirit that he got when he was converted, he got from a new life and a new nature, and they could not lay that away in the grave. They could not bury it—it flew to meet its Maker. It may be that he is not satisfied, and will not be until the resurrection, but Christ says: "*He shall see the travail of his soul, and shall be satisfied*" (Isaiah 53:11). Even the body will be raised; this body, sown in dishonor, will be raised in glory. This body, which has put on corruption, will put on incorruption, and this mortal will put on immortality. It is only a question of time. The great morning of the world will, by and by, dawn on the earth, and the dead will come forth and hear the voice of Him who is the resurrection and the life.

Paul said:

If our earthly house of this tabernacle were dissolved, we have a building of God, a house not made with hands, eternal in the heavens.

(2 Corinthians 5:1)

He could take down the clay temple, and leave that if he had a better house. He said in one place:

I am in a strait betwixt two, having a desire to depart, and to be with Christ, which is far better; nevertheless to abide in the flesh is more needful for you. (Philippians 1:23–24)

To me, it is sweet to think that death does not separate us from the Master. A great many people are living continually in the bondage of death, but if I have eternal life, death cannot touch that. It may touch the house I live in; it may change my countenance and send my body away to the grave, but it cannot touch this new life. To me, it is very sad to think that so many professed Christians look upon death as they do.

Some time ago, I received a letter from a friend in London, and I thought that I would take it and read it to other people to see if I could get them to view death as this friend did. He lost a loved mother. In England it is a very common thing to send out cards in memory of the departed ones. They put great borders of black on the cards—sometimes a quarter of an inch of black border—but this friend had gone and put on gold. She had gone to the golden city, and so he just put on a golden border. I think it is a good deal better than black. I think when our friends die, instead of putting a great black border on our memorials to make them look dark, it would be a better idea for us to put on gold.

It is not death at all; it is life. Someone said to a person dying, "Well, you are in the land of the living yet." "No," said he, "I am in the land of the dying yet, but I am going to the land of the living; they live there and never die." This is the land of sin and death and tears, but up yonder they never die. It is perpetual life; it is unceasing joy! "It is a glorious thing to die" was the testimony of Hannah More on her deathbed, though her life had been sown thick with the rarest friendships. Age had not so weakened her memory as to cause her to forget those little hamlets among the cliffs of her native hills, or the mission schools she had with such perseverance established, and where she would be so deeply missed.

Knowing Our Friends

Many are anxious to know if they will recognize their friends in heaven. In Matthew 8:11, we read:

> *And I say unto you, That many shall come from the east and west, and shall sit down with Abraham, and Isaac, and Jacob, in the kingdom of heaven.*

Here we find that Abraham, who lived so many hundreds of years before Christ, had not lost his identity. Christ tells us that the time is coming when they will come from the east and west and sit down with Abraham, Isaac, and Jacob in the kingdom of God. These men have not lost their identities—they are still known as Abraham, Isaac, and Jacob. And if you will turn to that wonderful scene that took place on the Mount of Transfiguration, you will find that Moses, who had been gone from the earth 1,500 years, was there. Peter, James, and John saw him on the Mount of Transfiguration. They saw him as Moses; he had not lost his name. (See Matthew 17.) God says in Isaiah, *"I will not blot your names out of the Lamb's Book of Life."* We have names in heaven. We are going to bear our names there—we will be known.

Psalm 17:15 says, *"I shall be satisfied, when I awake, with thy likeness."* That is enough. Want is written on every human heart down here, but in heaven we will be satisfied. You may hunt the world from one

45

end to the other, and you will not find a man or woman who is satisfied. But in heaven we will want for nothing. It says in 1 John 3:2–3, speaking to followers of Christ:

> *Beloved, now are we the sons of God, and it doth not yet appear what we shall be: but we know that, when he shall appear, we shall be like him; for we shall see him as he is. And every man that hath this hope in him purifieth himself, even as he is pure.*

It seems highly probable, indeed, I think it is clearly taught by Scripture, that a great many careless Christians will get into heaven. There will be a great many who will get in by the skin of their teeth, or as Lot was saved from Sodom, so as by fire. They will barely get in, but there will be no crown of rejoicing.

But *everybody* is not going to rush into heaven. There are a great many who *won't* be there. You know, we have a class of people who tell us they are going into the kingdom of God, whether they are converted or not. They tell us that they are on their way; that they are going there. They tell us everyone is going there. They believe that the good, the bad, and the indifferent are all going into the kingdom. They say that there is no difference, and, in other words—if I may be allowed to use plain language—they make God a liar. But they say, "We believe in the *mercy* of God"; so do I. I believe in the *justice* of God, too, and I think heaven would be a good deal worse than this earth if an unrenewed man were permitted to go into it. Why, if a man should live forever in this world in sin, what would become of this world? It seems as if it would be *hell itself.*

Let your mind review the history of this country and think of some who have lived in it. Suppose they never die. Suppose they live on and on forever in sin and rebellion. Do you think that God is going to welcome in those men who have rejected His Son, who have rejected the offer of His mercy, who have rejected salvation, who have trampled His law under their feet, and have been in rebellion against His laws down here? Do you suppose God is going to take them right into His kingdom and let them live there forever? By no means!

No Saloons in Heaven

No drunkard will inherit the kingdom of heaven. Now, let those mothers whose children are beginning a frivolous life wake up! Do not rest day or night until your children are converted by the power of God's grace, because no drunkard will inherit the kingdom of God. These moderate drinkers will become drunkards; no person ever became a drunkard all at once. How the devil blinds these moderate drinkers! I do not know of any sin more binding than the sin of alcoholism; the person is bound hand and foot before he knows it.

Some time ago, I was reading an account of snake-worshipping in India. I thought it was a horrible thing. I read of a mother who saw a snake come into her home and coil itself around her little six-month-old infant. She thought that the reptile was such a sacred thing that she did not dare to touch it. She watched that snake destroy her child.

She heard her baby's pitiful cries, but dared not rescue it. My soul revolted as I read it. But I do not know that we don't have things right here in America that are just as bad as that serpent in India. Serpents are coming into many Christian homes, coiling around many children and binding them hand and foot, and the fathers and mothers seem to be asleep.

O, may the Spirit of God wake us up! No drunkard will inherit the kingdom of God. Bear it in mind. "*Woe unto him that givest his neighbor drink*" (Habakkuk 2:15). I pity any professed Christians who rent their property for drinking saloons. I pity them from the depths of my heart. If you ever expect to inherit the kingdom of God, give it up. If you can never rent your property to better purpose, you had better let it stand empty. The idea that all is going well, and that all are going into the kingdom of God, whether they repent or not, is not taught anywhere in Scripture.

There will be no extortioners in heaven, those men that are just taking advantage of their brothers. They take advantage of those who have been unfortunate, whose families are sick, and who have had to go and mortgage their property. They make snap judgments against these poor souls and take every cent that they can get their hands on. These men are extortioners. They will not inherit the kingdom of God. I pity a man who acquires money dishonestly. See the trouble that he has in keeping it. It is sure to be scattered. If you got it dishonestly, you can't keep it. Your children can't keep it—they haven't got the power. You see that all over the country. A man who gets a dollar dishonestly had better make restitution and pay it back very quickly, or it will burn in his pocket.

Some Won't Get In

In the days of Noah, we read that he made it through the flood. He was the only righteous man. But, according to the theory of some people, the rest of those men who were so foul and so wicked—too wicked to live—God just took and swept them all into heaven. He left the only righteous man to go through this trial. Drunkards, thieves, and vagabonds all went to heaven, they say. You might as well go forward and preach, "You can swear as much as you like, and murder as much as you have a mind to, and it will all come out right—God will forgive you; God is so merciful."

Suppose the governor of a state pardons every person that the courts ever convicted, who are now lying in its jails and penitentiaries. Suppose he lets them all loose because he is so merciful that he could not bear to have men punished. I think he would not be governor of that state for very long. These men who are talking about God being so full of mercy—that He is going to spare all and take all men to heaven—would be the very men to say that such a governor as that ought to be impeached. They would say that he should not be governor. Let us bear in mind that Scripture says there is a certain class of people who will not inherit the kingdom of God. Now, I will give you the Scripture. It is a good deal better to just give the Scripture for these things, and then if you don't like it, you can quarrel with Scripture, and not with me. Let no man say that I have been saying who is going to heaven and who is not. I will let the Scripture speak for itself: *"Know ye not that the unrighteous shall not inherit the kingdom of God"* (1 Corinthians 6:9).

But the unrighteous—the adulterers, the fornicators, and the thieves—these people may all inherit it if they will only turn away from their sins. *"Let the wicked forsake his way, and the unrighteous man his thoughts"* (Isaiah 55:7). But if the unrighteous man says, "I will not turn away from sin; I will hold on to sin and have heaven," he is deceiving himself.

A man who steals my wallet loses a good deal more than I do. I can afford to let him have my wallet a great deal more than he can afford to take it. See how much that man loses when he steals my wallet. Perhaps he may get a few dollars—or he may steal my coat—but he does not get very much. See how much he has lost. Take an inventory of what that man loses if he loses heaven. Think of it. No thief will inherit the kingdom of God. To any thief I would say: steal no more. Let him ask God to forgive him. Let him repent of his sin and turn to God. If you get eternal life, it is worth more than the whole world. If you were to steal the whole world, you wouldn't get much, after all. The whole world does not amount to much, if you do not have eternal life with it, to enjoy yourself in the future.

Chapter 3

HEAVEN...ITS HAPPINESS

"What! Almost home?" "Yes, almost home," she said,
And light seemed gleaming on her aged head.
"Jesus is very precious!" Those who near
Her bedside stood were thrilled those words to hear.
"Toward His blest home I turn my willing feet;
Hinder me not; I go my Lord to meet."
Silence ensued. She seemed to pass away,
Serene and quiet as that summer day.

"Speak," cried through tears her daughter, bending low,
"One word, beloved mother, ere you go."
She spoke that word; the last she spoke on earth,
In whispering tones—that word of wondrous worth:
"Jesus!" The sorrowing listeners caught the sound,
But angels heard it with a joy profound.

HEAVEN...ITS HAPPINESS

If there is one name above any other that will swing open the eternal gates, it is the name of Jesus. There are a great many passwords and bywords down here, but that will be the countersign up above. Jesus Christ is the "open sesame" to heaven. Anyone who tries to climb up some other way is a thief and a robber. But when we get in, what a joy above every other joy we can think of—to see Jesus Himself, and to be with Him continually.

Isaiah has given this promise of God to everyone who is saved through faith: "*Thine eyes shall see the king in his beauty: they shall behold the land that is very far off*" (Isaiah 33:17). Some of us may not be able to travel around the world. We may not be able to see any of the foreign countries, but every Christian by and by is going to see a land that is very far off. This is our Promised Land. John Milton, the poet, says of the saints who have already gone:

> They walk with God
> High in salvation,
> and the climes of bliss.

There is a blissful climate up there. People down here search for a good climate where they won't be troubled by any of their pains or aches. Well, the climate of heaven is so fine that no pains or aches can hold out against it. There will be no room to find fault. We will leave all our pains and aches behind us and find an everlasting health, such as earth can never know.

But you know, the glory of Christ as reigning King of heaven would be too much for *mortal* eyes to stand. In 1 Timothy 6:15–16, we read of Christ as,

> *The blessed and only Potentate, the Kings of kings, and Lord of lords; Who only hath immortality, dwelling in the light which no man can approach unto; whom no man hath seen, nor can see.*

As mortals, we cannot see that light. Our feeble faculties would be dazzled before such a blaze of glory. In Ezekiel 8:28, we find where that prophet had a faint glimpse of it,

> *As the appearance of the bow that is in the cloud in the day of rain, so was the appearance of the brightness round about. This was the appearance of the likeness of the glory of the Lord. And when I saw it, I fell upon my face.*

We are amazed at ordinary perfections now. Few of us can look the sun square in the face. But when this corruptible body has put on incorruption, as Paul said, the powers of the soul will be stronger. (See 1 Corinthians 15:54.) We will be able to see Christ in His glory then. Though the moon be confounded and the sun ashamed, yet will we see Him as He is. (See Isaiah 24:23.) This is what will make heaven so happy. We all know that great happiness cannot be found on earth. Reason, revelation, and the experience of history all tell us that. No human creature has the power to give it. Even doing good fails to give it right away. For, owing to sin in the world, even the best do not have perfect happiness here. They have to wait for heaven, although they may be so near it sometimes that they can see heralds of its joy and beauty, like Columbus saw the strange and beautiful birds hovering around his ships long before he caught sight of America.

All the joys we are to know in heaven will come from the presence of God. This is the leading thought in all that Scripture has to say on the subject. What life on this earth is without health, life in heaven would be without the presence of God. God's presence will be the very light and life of the place. It is said that one translation of the words describing the presence of God is "a happy making sight." It will be a sight like the return of a long-lost boy to his mother or the first glimpse of your home after you have been away for a long time. Some of you know how a little sunshine on a dark day, or the face of a kind friend in trouble, often cheers you up. Well, heaven will be something like that, only a thousand times better. Our perception of God will be clearer then, and that will make us love Him all the more.

The more we know God, the more we love Him. A great many of us would love God more if we only got better acquainted. It gives Christians on earth a great deal of pleasure to think of the perfection of Jesus Christ. But, how will it be when we see Him as He is?

We Will Be Like Him

Someone once asked a Christian what he expected to do when he got to heaven. He said he expected to spend the first thousand years looking at Jesus Christ, and after that he would look for Peter, and then for James and John. And, all the time he could conceive of would be joyfully filled with looking on these great persons. But it seems to me that one look at Jesus Christ will more than reward us for all we have ever done for Him down here. Just to see Him will be more than sufficient for all the sacrifices we can possibly make for Him. But, even more, we will become like Him when we see Him—we will have His Spirit. Jesus, the Savior of the world, will be there, and we will see Him face-to-face.

It won't be the pearly gates, it won't be the jasper walls, or the streets paved with transparent gold, that will make it heaven to us. These would not satisfy us. If these were all, we would not want to stay there forever. I heard of a child whose mother was very sick. While she lay very low, one of the neighbors took the child away to stay with her until the mother was well again. But instead of getting better, the mother died. They decided they would not take the child home until the funeral was all over, and would never tell her about her mother being dead. So, after a while, they brought the little girl home. First she went in the sitting room to find her mother; then she went into the parlor to find her mother there. She went from one end of the house to the other and could not find her.

At last she said, "Where is my mama?" And when they told her that her mama was gone, the little thing wanted to go back to the neighbor's house again. Home had lost its attraction to her since her mother was not there any longer. No, it's not the jasper walls

61

or the pearly gates that are going to make heaven attractive. It is being with God. We will be in the presence of the Redeemer; we will be forever with the Lord.

There was a time when I used to think more of Jesus Christ than I did of the Father. Christ seemed to be so much nearer to me because He had become the link between myself and God. In my imagination I put God away on the throne as a stern judge. But Christ had come in as the meditator, and it seemed as if Chirst was much nearer to me than God the Father. I got over that years ago when God gave me a son. For ten years I had an only son, and as I looked at the child as he grew up, the thought came to me that it took more love for God to give up His Son than it did for His Son to die. It would be much easier for me to go out and be put to death than to see the son of my bosom—my only son—led out and crucified. Think of the love that God had for this world when He gave Christ up!

If you will turn to Acts 7:55, you will find that when Stephen was being stoned he lifted up his eyes, and it seemed as if God just rolled back the curtain of time, allowing him to look into the eternal city, and see Christ standing at the right hand of God. When Jesus Christ went on high, He led captivity captive and took His seat, for His work was done. But when Stephen saw Jesus, He was standing up, and I can imagine He saw that martyr fighting, as it were, single-handed and alone—the first martyr, though many were to come after him. You can hear the tramp of the millions coming after him to lay down their lives for the Son of God. But Stephen led the way. He was the first martyr, and as he was dying for the Lord Jesus Christ, he looked up. Christ was standing to give him a welcome, and the Holy Spirit came down to bear witness that Christ was there. How then can we doubt it?

A beggar does not enjoy looking at a palace. The grandeur of its architecture is lost on him. Looking at a royal banquet does not satisfy the hunger of a starving man. But seeing heaven is also having a share in it. There would be no joy there if we did not feel that some of it was ours. God unites the soul to Himself. As it says in 2 Peter 1:4, we are made partakers of the divine nature. Now, if you put a piece of iron in the fire it soon loses its dark color, and it becomes red and hot like the fire; but it does not lose its iron nature. So the soul becomes bright with God's brightness, beautiful with God's beauty, pure with God's purity, and warm with the glow of His perfect love, and yet remains a human soul. We will be like Him, but remain ourselves.

There is a fable of a kindhearted king who was once hunting in a forest and found a blind orphan boy who was living almost like the beasts. The king was touched with pity, adopted the boy as his own, and had him taught all that can be learned by one who is blind. When the boy had his twenty-first year, the king, who was also a great physician, restored to the youth his sight. He then took him to his palace where, surrounded by his nobles and all the majesty and magnificence of his court, he proclaimed him one of his sons, and commanded all to give him their honor and love. The once friendless orphan thus became a prince and a sharer in the royal dignity, the happiness, and the glory to be found in the palace of the king. Who can know the joy that overwhelmed the soul of that young man when he first saw the king of whose beauty, goodness, and power he had heard so much? Who can know the happiness he must have felt when he saw his own princely attire, and found himself adopted into the royal family—honored and loved by all?

Now, Christ is the great and mighty King who finds our souls in the wilderness of this sinful world. He finds us, as it says in Revelation, *"wretched, and miserable, and poor, and blind, and naked"* (Revelation 3:17). He *"washed us from our sins in His own blood"* (Revelation 1:5). It also says in Isaiah 61:10:

> *He hath clothed me with the garments of salvation, he hath covered me with the robe of righteousness, as a bridegroom decketh himself with*

*ornaments, and as a bride adorneth
herself with jewels.*

The mission of the gospel to sinners, as
we find it in Acts 26:18, has been,

*To open their eyes, and to turn them
from darkness to light, and from the
power of Satan unto God, that they
may receive forgiveness of sins, and
inheritance among them which are
sanctified by faith that is in me.*

This is what Christ has done for every
Christian. He has adorned you with the gift
of grace and adopted you as His child and,
as it says,

*All things are yours; whether Paul,
or Apollos, or Cephas, or the world,
or life, or death, or things present, or
things to come; all are yours; and ye
are Christ's and Christ is God's.*

(1 Corinthians 3:21–23)

He has given you His own Word to edu-
cate you for heaven; He has opened your eyes
so that now you see. By His grace and your
cooperation, your soul is being gradually

developed into a more perfect resemblance of Him. Finally, your heavenly Father calls you home, where you will see the angels and saints clothed with the beauty of Christ Himself. You will see them standing around His throne, and hear the word that will admit you into their society: *"Well done good and faithful servant...enter thou into the joy of thy Lord"* (Matthew 25:23). Christ Himself says, *"All things that the Father hath are mine: therefore said I, that he shall take of mine, and shall show it unto you"* (John 16:15). All will be yours. Ah, how poor and mean do earthly pleasures seem by comparison.

Over the River

There is joy in heaven, we are told, over the conversions that take place on earth. In Luke 15:7, we read:

> *I say unto you, that likewise joy shall be in heaven over one sinner that repenteth, more than over ninety and nine just persons, which need no repentance.*

If there was going to be an election for the president of the United States, there would be tremendous excitement—a great commotion. There is probably not a paper from Maine to California that would not have something on nearly every page about the candidate. The whole country would be excited. But I doubt if it would be noticed in heaven. I doubt if they would take any notice of it at all. If the Queen of England should leave her throne, there would be great excitement throughout the nations of the earth. The whole world would be interested in the event. It would be telegraphed around the world; but it would probably be altogether overlooked in heaven. Yet, if one little boy or one little girl, one man or one woman, should repent of their sins, this day and hour would be noticed in heaven. They look at things differently up there—things that look very large to us look very small in heaven. And, things that seem very small to us down here may be very great up yonder. Think of it! By an act of our own, we may cause joy in heaven. The thought seems almost too wonderful to take in. To think that the poorest sinner on earth, by an act of his own, can send a thrill of joy through the hosts of heaven!

The Bible says, *"There is joy in the presence of the angels,"* not that the angels rejoice, but it is *"in the presence"* of the angels (Luke 15:10). I had studied over that a great deal, and often wondered what it meant. *"Joy in the presence of the angels"*? Now, it is speculation, it may be true or it may not, but perhaps the friends who have left the shores of time—those who have gone within the fold—may be looking down upon us. And, when they see one they prayed for while on earth repenting and turning to God, it sends a thrill of joy to their very hearts. Even now, some mother who has gone up yonder may be looking down on a son or daughter, and if that child should say, "I will meet that mother of mine. I will repent. Yes, I am going to join you, Mother," the news, with the speed of a sunbeam, reaches heaven. And, that mother may then rejoice, as we read, *"In the presence of the angels."*

In Dublin, a man walked into the prayer room with his daughter—his only one—whose mother had died some time before, and he prayed, "Oh God, let this truth go deep into my daughter's heart, and grant that the prayers of her mother may be answered today—that she maybe saved." As they rose up, she put her arms around his neck, kissed him, and said, "I want to meet my mother. I want to be a Christian." That day she accepted Christ. That man is now a minister in Texas. The daughter died out there a little while ago, and is now with her mother in heaven. What a blessed and joyful meeting it must have been! It may be a sister, it may be a brother, who is beckoning you over—

Over the river they beckon to me,
Loved ones who've crossed to the farther side;
The gleam of their snowy robes I see,
But their voices are drowned in the rushing tide.
There's one with ringlets of sunny gold,
And eyes, the reflection of heaven's own blue;
He crossed in the twilight gray and cold,
And the pale mist hid him from mortal view.
We saw not the angels who met him there,
The gates of the city we could not see;
Over the river, over the river,
My brother stands waiting to welcome me.

Whoever it is, do not delay.

There is a story about a father who had his little daughter out late in the evening. The night was dark, and they had passed through a thick woods to the edge of a river. Far away on the opposite shore a light twinkled here and there in the few scattered houses. Farther off still blazed the bright lamps of the great city to which they were going. The little child was weary and sleepy, and the father held her in his arms while he waited for the ferryman, who was at the other side. At length, they saw a little light; nearer and nearer came the sound of the oars, and soon they were safe in the boat.

"Father," said the little girl.

"Well, my child?"

"It's very dark, and I can't see the shore. Where are we going?"

"The ferryman knows the way, little one; we will soon be over."

"O, I wish we were there, Father!"

Soon in her home, loving arms welcomed her, and her fears and her tremor were gone.

71

Some months pass by, and this same little child stands on the edge of a river that is darker and deeper, more terrible still. It is the river of death. The same loving father stands near her, distressed that his child must cross this river and he not able to go with her. For days and nights, he and her mother have been watching over her, leaving her bedside only long enough for their meals, and to pray for the life of their precious one. For hours, she has been slumbering, and it seems as if her spirit must pass away without her waking again. But, just before the morning watch, she suddenly awakes with bright eyes, a clear mind, and every faculty alive. A sweet smile is playing on her face.

"Father," she says, "I have come again to the riverside, and am again waiting for the ferryman to come and take me across."

"Does it seem as dark and cold as when you went over the other river, my child?"

"Oh no! There is no darkness here. The river is covered with floating silver. The boat coming toward me seems made of solid light, and I am not afraid of the ferryman."

"Can you see over the river, my darling?"

"Oh yes, there is a great and beautiful city there, all filled with light. And, I hear music such as the angels make!"

"Do you see anyone on the other side?"

"Why yes, yes, I see the most beautiful form. And He beckons me now to come. Oh ferryman, make haste! I know who it is! It is Jesus, my own blessed Jesus. I will be caught in His arms. I will rest on His bosom—I come—I *come.*"

And thus she crossed over the river of death, made like a silver stream by the presence of the blessed Redeemer.

Something More

Almost every man, no matter how high up or how rich he may be, will tell you (if you gain his confidence) that he is unhappy. There is something he wants that he cannot get, or there is something he has that he wants to get rid of. It is very doubtful if the leader of Russia is a happy man, and yet he has about all he can get. Although the Queen of England has castles and millions at her command, and has besides what most sovereigns lack—the love of her subjects—it is questionable whether or not she gets much pleasure out of her position. If they love the Lord Jesus Christ and are saved, then they may be happy. If they know they will get into heaven like the humblest of their subjects, then they may rest secure. Paul, the humble tentmaker, will have a higher seat in heaven than the best and greatest sovereign that ever ruled the earth. If the Russian leader should meet John Bunyan, the poor tinker, up in heaven, he no doubt would find him the greater man.

The Christian life is the only happy one. Something is always lacking, otherwise. When we are young, we have grand enterprises, but we soon spoil them by being too rash. We lack experience. When we get old, we have the experience, but then all the power to carry out our schemes is gone. *"Happy is that people, whose God is the Lord"* (Psalm 144:15). The only way to be happy is to be good. The man who steals out of necessity sins because he is afraid of being unhappy—but for the moment he forgets all about how unhappy the sin is going to make him. Man is the best and noblest thing on earth, as bad as he is, and it is easy to understand how he fails to find true happiness in anything lower than himself. The only object better than ourselves is God, and He is all we can ever be satisfied with. Gold, mere waste dug up out of the earth, does not satisfy man. Neither does the honor and praise of other men. The human soul wants something more than that, and heaven is the only place to get it. No wonder the angels who see God all the time are so happy.

The tax collectors looked for John the Baptist in the wilderness to find out what they should do. Some of the highest men in the land went out to consult the hermit to know how to get happiness. *"Whoso trusteth in the Lord, happy is he"* (Proverbs 16:20). It is because there is *no* real happiness down here, and earth is not worth living for. It is because it is all above that heaven is worth dying for. In heaven, there is all life and no death. In hell, there is all death and no life. Here on earth, there is both living and dying, which is between the two. If we are dead to sin here, we will live in heaven; and if we live in sin here, we must expect eternal death to follow.

Do you know that every converted sinner dies twice? He first becomes spiritually dead to sin—that is the renewed soul. The soul then begins to feel the joy of heaven. The joys of heaven reach down to earth as many and as sure as the rays of the sun. Then comes physical death, which makes way for the physical heaven. Of course, the old, sinful body has to be left behind. We cannot take that into heaven. We will receive a glorified body at the resurrection, not a sinful body. Our bodies will be transfigured like Christ's.

Besides, there will be no temptation then. If there was no temptation in the world now, God could not test us. He wants to see if we are loyal. That is why He put the forbidden tree in Paradise—that accounts for the Canaanites in Israel. When we plant a seed, after a time it disappears and brings forth a seed that looks much the same, but still it is a different seed. So our bodies and the bodies of those we know and love will be raised up, looking much the same but still not all the same. Christ took the same body into heaven that was crucified on the cross, unless He was transformed in the cloud after the disciples lost sight of Him.

There must have been some change in the appearance of Christ after His resurrection, for Mary Magdalene, who was the first one who saw Him, did not know Him. Neither did the disciples, who walked and talked with Him about Himself, recognize Him until He began to ask a blessing at supper. Even Peter did not know Him when He appeared on the seashore. Thomas would not believe it was Christ until he saw the scars of the nails and the wound in His side. But we will all know Him in heaven.

There are two things that the Bible makes as clear and certain as eternity. One is that we are going to see Christ, and the other is that we are going to be like Him. God will never hide His face from us there, and Satan will never show his. There is not such a great difference between grace and glory after all. Grace is the bud, and glory the blossom. Grace is glory begun, and glory is grace perfected. It won't come hard to people who are serving God down here to do it when they go up yonder. They will change places, but they won't change employments.

Higher Up

The moment a person becomes heavenly-minded and gets his heart and affections on things above, then life becomes beautiful. The light of heaven shines across out pathway and we don't have to be upbraiding ourselves all the time because we do not spend more time with Christ. Someone asked a Scotsman if he was on the way to heaven, and he said, "Why, man, I live there; I am not on the way." Now we want to live in heaven; while we are walking in this world it is our privilege to have our hearts and affections there.

There is a place in Chicago, and has been for years, where a great many Christians have always gone when they want to get their faith strengthened. They go there and visit one of the bedridden but holy saints. A friend told me that she thought that the Lord kept one of those saints in most of the cities to entertain angels as they passed over on errands of mercy, for it seems that these saints are often visited by the heavenly host.

I once heard Mr. Morehouse, the American author, tell a story about a woman missionary in London who found one of those poor, bedridden saints. Then the missionary found a wealthy woman who was always complaining and murmuring at her lot. Sometimes I think people for whom God does the most in worldly ways think less of Him, care less about Him, and are the most unproductive in His service. At any rate, this missionary woman went around visiting the poor, and she used to go and visit this poor, bedridden saint. She said if she wanted to be cheered up and her heart made happy, she would go and visit her. Well, this woman missionary had wanted to introduce the wealthy woman to this saint. She invited her to go a number of times, and finally the lady consented. When she got to the place, she went up the first flight of stairs, and it was dark and not very clean.

"What a horrible place," the lady said. "Why did you bring me here?"

The missionary smiled and said, "It is better higher up."

They went up another flight, and it didn't grow any lighter. She complained again, and the lady said, "It is better higher up." Then they went up another flight and it was still no lighter, and the missionary kept saying, "It is better higher up." When they got to the fifth story, they opened the door and entered into a beautiful room—a room that was carpeted, with plants in the window, and a little bird in a cage singing. There was that saint just smiling, and the first thing the complaining woman had to say to her was, "It must be hard for you to be here and suffer."

"Oh, that is a very small thing; it is not very hard," she said. "It is better higher up."

And so if things don't go just right, if they don't suit us here, we can say, "It's better higher up; it is better further on." We can lift up our hearts and rejoice as we journey on toward home.

Chapter 4

HEAVEN...ITS CERTAINTY

O friends of mortal years,
The trusted and the true,
Ye are watching still in the valley of tears,
But I wait to welcome you.

Why should your tears tun down,
And your hearts be sorely given,
For another gem in the Savior's crown,
And another soul in heaven!

HEAVEN...ITS CERTAINTY

There are some people who trust their reason so much that they reason away God. They say God is not a person whom we can ever see. They say God is a spirit. So He is, but He is a person too—He became a man and walked the earth once. Scripture tells us very plainly that God has a dwelling place. There is no doubt whatsoever about that. A dwelling place indicates personality. God's dwelling place is in heaven. He has a dwelling place, and we are going to be inmates of it. Therefore, we will see Him.

In 1 Kings 8:30 we read:

And hearken thou to the supplication of thy servant, and of thy people Israel, when they shall pray toward this place: and hear thou in heaven thy dwelling place: and when thou hearest, forgive.

This idea that heaven is everywhere and nowhere is not according to Scripture.

Heaven is God's habitation, and when Christ came on earth He taught us to pray: "Our Father which art in heaven." This habitation is called "the city of eternal life."

Think of a city without a cemetery—they have no dying there. If there could be such a city as that found on this earth, what a rush there would be to it! How men would seek to get into that city! You can't find one on the face of this earth. A city without tears—God wipes away all the tears up yonder. This is a time of weeping, but, by and by, there is a time coming when God will call us where there will be no tears. A city without pain, without sorrow, without sickness, without death. There is no darkness there. The Lamb is the light thereof. It needs no sun; it needs no moon. The paradise of Eden was nothing compared to this one. The tempter came into Eden and triumphed, but in that city, nothing that defiles will ever enter. There will be no tempter there. Think of a place where temptation cannot come. Think of a place where we will be free from sin, where pollution cannot enter, and where the righteous will reign forever. Think of a city that is not built with hands, where the buildings do not grow old with time. Think of a city whose inhabitants no census has numbered except the Book of Life, which is the heavenly directory. Think of a city through whose streets runs no tide of business, where no nodding hearses creep slowly with their burdens to the tomb. Think of a city without griefs or graves, without sins or sorrows, without marriages or mournings, without births or burials. Think of a city which glories in having Jesus for its King, angels for its guards, and whose citizens are saints!

We believe this is just as much a place and just as much a city as New York is, or London or Paris. We believe in it a great deal more, because earthly cities will pass away, but this city will remain forever. It has foundations whose builder and maker is God. Some of the grandest cities the world has ever known did not have foundations strong enough to last.

Our Names Recorded

We are told that one time, just before sunrise, two men got into a dispute about what part of the heavens the sun would appear in first. They became so excited over it that they began fighting. They beat each other over the head so badly that when the sun did come up, neither of them could see it. So there are people who go on disputing about heaven until they dispute themselves *out* of it. There are even more people who dispute over hell until they dispute themselves *into* it.

In their writings, the Hebrews tell us of three distinct heavens. The air, the wind—the place where the birds fly—is one heaven. The atmosphere where the stars are is another. And above that is the heaven of heavens, where God's throne is, and the mansions of the Lord are—those mansions of light and peace which are the abode of the blessed, the home of the Redeemer and the redeemed. This is the heaven where Christ is. This is the place we read of where it says, *"Behold, the heaven and the heaven of heavens is the Lord's thy God, the earth also, with all that therein is"* (Deuteronomy 10:14).

Paul, speaking for himself, said:

*I knew a man in Chirst above four-
teen years ago, (whether in the body, I
cannot tell; or whether out of the body,
I cannot tell: God knoweth;) such an
one caught up to the third heaven.*
(2 Corinthians 12:2)

Some people have wondered what that
third heaven means. That is where God
dwells, and where the storms do not come.
There sits the incorruptible Judge. Paul,
when he was caught up there, heard things
that were not lawful for him to utter, and he
saw things that he could not speak of down
here. The higher up we get in spiritual mat-
ters, the nearer we seem to heaven. There
our wishes are fulfilled at last. We may cry
out like the psalmist:

*One thing have I desired of the Lord,
that will I seek after; that I may dwell
in the house of the Lord all the days
of my life, to behold the beauty of the
Lord.* (Psalm 27:4)

We are assured by Christ Himself that
our names will be written in heaven if
we are only His. In Luke 10:20 it reads,

"Notwithstanding in this rejoice not, that the spirits are subject unto you; but rather rejoice, because your names are written in heaven." A little while before these words were uttered by the Savior—calling together seventy of His disciples—He sent them forth in pairs to preach the gospel to all men. There are people nowadays who have no faith in revivals. Yet the greatest revival the world ever saw was during the three or four years that John the Baptist and Jesus were preaching, followed by the preaching of the apostles and disciples after Christ left the earth. For years, the country was stirred from one end to the other. There were probably men then who stood out against the revival. They called it spasmodic and refused to believe in it. It was a nine days' wonder and would pass away in a little while. There would be nothing left of it.

No doubt men talked in those days just as they talk now. All the way down from the time of Christ and His apostles, there have been men who have opposed the work of God—some of them professing to be disciples of the Lord Jesus Christ—all because it has not been done in their way. When the Spirit of God comes, He works in His own way. We must learn not to mark out any channels for Him to work in, for He will work in His own way when He comes.

These disciples came back after their work. The Spirit had worked with them; the devils were subject to them; they had power over disease; they had power over the enemy; and they were filled with success. They were probably having a sort of praise meeting when Christ came in and said, *"Rejoice not, that the spirits are subject unto you; but rather rejoice, because your names are written in heaven"* (Luke 10:20). This brings us face-to-face with the doctrine of assurance. I find a great many people throughout Christendom who do not accept this doctrine. They believe it is impossible for us to know in this life whether we are saved or not. If this is true, how are we going to explain what Christ has said as we find it here recorded? If my name is written in heaven, how can I rejoice over it unless I know it? These men were to rejoice that their names were already there, and whoever are children of God, *their* names are there, sent on for registry beforehand.

A few years ago, a party of Americans on their way from London to Liverpool decided that they would stop at the Northwestern Hotel. But when they arrived, they found the place had been full for several days. Greatly disappointed, they took up their baggage and were about to leave when they noticed a lady of the party preparing to remain.

"Are you not going, too?" they asked.

"Oh no," she said, "I have good rooms all ready."

"Why, how did that happen?"

"Oh," she said, "I telegraphed ahead a few days ago."

Now, that is what the children of God are doing—they are sending their names on ahead. They are securing places in the mansions of Christ in time. If we are truly children of God, our names have gone on beforehand, and there will be places awaiting us at the end of the journey. You know we are only travelers down here. We are away from home. When the Civil War was going on, the soldiers on the battlefield—the Southern soldiers and the Northern soldiers—wanted nothing better to live in than tents. They longed for the war to end so that they might go home. They did not care about having palaces or mansions on the battlefield. Well, there is a terrible battle going on now, and by and by, when the war is over, God will call us home. The tents and altars are good enough for us while journeying through this world. It is only a night, and then the eternal day will dawn.

The Book of Life

Two ladies met on a train not long ago, one of them going to Cairo, Georgia, and the other to New Orleans. Before they reached Cairo, they had formed a strong attachment for each other, and the Cairo lady said to the lady who was going to New Orleans, "I wish you would stay for a few days in Cairo; I would like to entertain you."

"Well," said the other, "I would like to very much, but I have packed up all my things and sent them ahead; I only brought what I have on, but they are good enough to travel in." I learned a lesson there. Almost anything is good enough to travel in, and it is a great deal better to have our joys and comforts ready for us in heaven—waiting until we get there—than to wear them out in our toilsome, trying, earthly journey.

Heaven is the place of victory and triumph. This is the battlefield; there is the triumphal procession. This is the land of the sword and the spear; that is the land of the wreath and the crown. Oh, what a thrill of joy will shoot through the hearts of all the blessed when their conquests will be made complete in heaven! How joyous the occasion when death itself, the last of foes, will be slain, and Satan dragged as captive at the chariot wheels of Christ! Men may quibble, laugh, and sneer as much as they want at this doctrine of assurance, but it is clearly taught in Scripture.

A great many laugh at the idea of there being books in heaven. But in Daniel 12:1 we find:

And at that time shall Michael stand up, the great prince which standeth for the children of thy people: and there shall be a time of trouble, such as never was since there was a nation even to that same time: and at that time thy people shall be delivered, every one that shall be found written in the book.

There is a terrible time coming upon this earth—darker days than we have ever seen—and those whose names are written in the Book of Life will be delivered. Then again, in Philippians 4:3 we read:

And I entreat thee also, true yokefellow, help those women which laboured with me in the gospel, with Clement also, and with other my fellowlabourers, whose names are in the book of life.

Paul, writing to the Christians at Philippi, where he had so much opposition, and where he was cast into jail, said in effect: Just take my regards to the good brethren who worked with me and whose names are written in the Book of Life. This shows that they taught the doctrine of assurance in the very earliest days of Christianity. Why should we not teach it and believe it now?

I am told by Eastern travelers—men who have been in China—that in their courts they have two great books. When a man is tried and found innocent, they write his name down in the book of life. If he is found guilty, they write his name down in the book of death. And I believe firmly that every man or woman has his or her name in the Book of Death or the Book of Life. Your name can't be in both books at the same time, and it is your own privilege to know which it is.

In Revelation 13:8 we read:

And all that dwell upon the earth shall worship him [the Anti-Christ], *whose names are not written in the book of life of the Lamb slain from the foundation of the world.*

Again in Revelation 20:12, we read:

And I saw the dead, small and great, stand before God; and the books were opened: and another book was opened, which is the book of life; and the dead were judged out of those things which were written in the books, according to their works.

Yet again in Revelation 21:27, we read:

And there shall in no wise enter into it any thing that defileth, neither whatsoever worketh abomination, or maketh a lie: but they which are written in the Lamb's book of life.

There can be no true peace, no true hope, no true comfort, where there is uncertainty. I am not fit for God's service, I cannot go out and work for God, if I am in doubt about my own salvation.

No Room for Doubt

A mother has a sick child. The child is just hanging between life and death. There is no rest for that mother. You have someone on a train that has wrecked, and the news comes that twenty have been killed and wounded. Their names are not given; there is a terrible uncertainty, and there is no rest or peace until you know the facts. The reason why there are so many in the churches who will not go out and help others is that they are not sure they are saved themselves. If I thought I was dying myself, I would be in a poor condition to save anyone else. Before I can pull anyone else out, I must have a firm footing on shore myself. We can have this complete assurance if we want it. It does not do to *feel* we are all right; we must *know* it. We must read our titles *clear* to mansions in the skies. The apostle John said, *"Beloved, now are we the sons of God"* (1 John 3:2). He did not say we are *going* to be.

People, when asked if they are Christians, give some of the strangest answers you have ever heard. Some will say, "Well—well—well, I—I hope I am." Suppose a man should ask me if I am an American, would I say, "Well, I—well, I—I hope I am"? I know that I was born in this country, and I know I was born of the Spirit of God more than twenty years ago. All the non-Christians in the world could not convince me that I do not have a different spirit than I had before I became a Christian. *"That which is born of the flesh is flesh; and that which is born of the Spirit is spirit"* (John 3:6), and a man can soon tell whether he is born of the Spirit by the change in his life. The spirit of Christ is a spirit of love, peace, joy, humility, and meekness, and we can soon find out whether we have been born of that spirit or not. We are not to be left in uncertainty. Job lived in the dark ages, but he knew. The dark billows came rolling and surging up against him, but in the midst of the storm you can hear his voice saying, *"I **know** that my redeemer liveth"* (Job 19:25, emphasis added). He did not guess.

A man may have his name written in the highest chronicles down here, but the record may be lost. He may have it carved in marble, and still it may perish. Some charitable institution may bear his name, and yet he may soon be forgotten. But his name will never be erased from the scrolls that are kept above. Seeking to perpetuate one's name on earth is like writing on the sand by the seashore. To be perpetual, it must be written on the eternal shores. No one thinks Pontius Pilate is a saint because he is mentioned in the Apostle's Creed. It has been said that the way to see our names as they stand written in the Book of Life is by reading the work of sanctification in our own hearts. It needs no miraculous voice from heaven, no extraordinary signs, no unusual feeling. We only need to find our hearts desiring Christ and hating sin—our minds obedient to the divine commands.

We may be sure that belonging to some church is not going to save us, although every saved man ought to be associated with one. When Daniel died in Babylon, no one had to hunt up any old church record to find out if he was all right. When Paul was beheaded by Nero, no one had to look over the register. They lived so that the world knew what they were. Paul said, *"I am persuaded that he is able to keep what I have committed unto him against that day"* (2 Timothy 1:12). *There* is assurance. *"Who shall separate us from the love of Christ?"* he said, *"neither death, not life, nor angels, nor principalities, nor powers, not things present, not things to come"* (Romans 8:35–38). He challenges them all, but they could not separate him from the love that was in Christ.

It is dishonoring to God to go on hoping and only hoping that we "are going" to be saved. Yet there *are* some who should not have assurance. It would be an unfortunate thing for any unconverted church member to have assurance. There are some who profess great assurance who should not have it—those whose lives do not correspond. This class is represented by the man at the wedding feast who did not have on a wedding garment.

False Professions

They are like some lilies—fair to see but foul to smell. They are dry shells with no kernel inside. The crusaders of old used to wear a painted cross on their shoulders. So there are a good many nowadays who take up crosses that sit lightly—mere things of ornament. They are as passports to respectability, cheap make-believes, for a struggle that has never been made, and a crown that has never been striven for.

You may very often see dead fish floating with the stream, but you never see a dead fish swimming against it. Well, that is your false believer; that is the hypocrite. Profession is just floating down the stream, but confession is swimming against it, no matter how strong the tide. The sanctified man and the unsanctified one look at heaven very differently. The unsanctified man simply chooses heaven in preference to hell. He thinks that if he must go to either one, he would rather try heaven. It is like a man with a farm, who has a place offered him in another country where there is said to be a gold mine. He hates to give up all he has and take any risk. But if he is going to be banished and must leave, and has his choice of living in a wilderness, digging in a coal pit, or taking the gold mine, then there is no hesitation. The unregenerate man likes heaven better than hell, but he likes this world the best of all. When death stares him in the face, then he thinks he would like to get to heaven. On the other hand, the true believer prizes heaven above everything else, and is always willing to give up the world. Everybody wants to enjoy heaven after they die, but they don't want to be heavenly minded while they live. To the Christian, it is a sure promise, and there is no room to doubt.

The heir to some great estate, while a child, thinks more of a dollar in his pocket than all his inheritance. So even some professing Christians sometimes are more elated by a passing pleasure than they are by their title to eternal glory. In a little while, we will be there. How glorious is the thought! Everything is prepared. That is what Christ went up to heaven for. In a little while, we will be gone.

Chapter 5

HEAVEN...ITS RICHES

Jerusalem, my Home,
Where shines the royal Throne,
Each king casts down his golden crown
Before the Lamb thereon.
Thence flows the crystal River,
And flowing on forever
With leaves and fruits on either hand,
The tree of Life shall stand.
In blood-washed robes, all white and fair,
The Lamb shall lead his chosen there,
While clouds of incense fill the air—
Jerusalem, my Home.

—Hopkins

HEAVEN...ITS RICHES

No man thinks of himself as being rich until he has all that he wants. Very few people are satisfied with earthly riches. If they want anything at all that they cannot get, that is a kind of poverty. Sometimes the richer the man, the greater the poverty. Somebody has said that getting riches brings care, keeping them brings trouble, abusing them brings guilt, and losing them brings sorrow.

It's a great mistake to make as much of riches as we do. But there are some riches that we cannot praise too highly. They never pass away. They are the treasures laid up in heaven for those who truly belong to God. No matter how rich or elevated we may be here, there is always something that we want. The greatest chance the rich have over the poor is the one they enjoy the least—that of making themselves happy. Worldly riches never make anyone truly happy. We all know, too, that they often take wings and fly away. Midas got gold, so that whatever he touched turned into it, but he was not much better off for it. There is a great deal of truth in some of these old fables. Money, like time, should not be wasted, but I pity the man who has more of either than he knows how to use. There is no truer saying than this: that man, by doing good with his money, stamps, as it were, the image of God on it, and makes it pass current for the merchandise of heaven. But, all the wealth of the universe would not buy a man's way there. Salvation must be taken as a gift for the asking. There is no man so poor that he may not be a heavenly millionaire.

A Bad Life Preserver

How many are worshipping gold today! Where war has slain its thousands, gold has slain its millions. Its history is the history of slavery and oppression in all ages. At this moment, what an empire it has. The mine with its drudgery, the factory with its misery, the plantation with its toil, and the market and exchange with their haggard and care-worn faces—these are only specimens of its menial servants. Titles and honors are its rewards, and thrones are at its disposal. Kings are its counselors, and many of the great and mighty of the earth are its subjects. This spirit of greed even tries to turn the globe itself into gold.

Tarpeia, the daughter of the governor of the fortress situated on the Capitoline Hill in Rome, was captivated by the golden bracelets of the Sabine soldiers, and she agreed to let them into the fortress if they would give her what they wore on their left arms. The contract was made; the Sabines kept their promise. Tatius, their commander, was the first to deliver his bracelets and shield. The coveted treasures were thrown on Tarpeia by each of the soldiers until she sank beneath their weight and died. Thus does the weight of gold carry many people downward.

When the steamship *Central America* went down, several hundred miners were on board, returning to their homes and friends. They had made their fortunes, and expected much happiness in enjoying them. When the ship began to sink, gold lost its attraction to them. The miners took off their treasure belts and threw them aside. Carpetbags full of shining gold dust were emptied onto the loot of the cabin. One of them poured out one hundred thousand dollars' worth in the cabin, and begged anyone who wanted it to take it. Greed was overmastered, and the gold found no takers. Dear friends! It is well enough to have gold, but sometimes it is a bad life preserver. Sometimes it is a mighty weight that crushes us down to hell.

One day, the Reverend John Newton of England visited a family that had suffered the loss of all they possessed by fire. He found the pious mistress and saluted her with, "I give you joy, Madam." Surprised, and ready to be offended, she exclaimed, "What! joy that all my property has been burned?" "Oh, no," he answered, "but joy that you have so much property that fire cannot touch." This allusion to her real treasures alleviated her grief and brought reconciliation. As it says in Proverbs 15:6, *"In the house of the righteous is much treasure: but in the revenues of the wicked is trouble."* I have never seen

a dying saint who was rich in heavenly treasures have any regrets. I have never heard
them say they had lived too much for God
and heaven.

Getting Water-Logged

A friend of mine says that he was at the
River Mersey in Liverpool when a vessel had
to be towed with a great deal of care into the
harbor. It was clear down to the water's edge,
and he wondered why it didn't sink. Pretty
soon another vessel came, without any help
at all. It didn't need any tug to tow it in, but
it sailed right up the Mersey past the other
vessels. He asked about it and found out that
the vessel that had to be towed in was what
they call waterlogged. It was loaded with
lumber and material of that sort, and having
sprung a leak, it had partially sunk. It was
very hard work to get it into the harbor.
Now, I believe there are a great many professed Christians, a great many perhaps who
are really Christians, who get waterlogged.
They have too many earthly treasures, and
it takes nearly the whole church—the whole
spiritual power of the church—to look after

these worldly Christians, to keep them from going back entirely into the world. Why, if the whole church were, as John Wesley said, "hard at it, and always at it," what a power there would be, and how soon we would teach the world and the masses. But, we are not reaching the world because the church itself has become conformed to the world and worldly minded. So many in the church are wondering why they don't grow in grace while they have more of the earth in their thoughts than God.

The ministers would not have to urge people to live for heaven if their treasures were up there. They could not help it—their hearts would be there, and if their hearts were there, their minds would be up there. Their life would center toward heaven. They could not help living for heaven if their treasures were there.

One day, a little girl said to her mother, "Mama, my Sunday school teacher tells me that this world is only a place in which God lets us live a while, so that we may prepare for a better world. But, Mother, I do not see anybody *preparing*. I see you preparing to go into the country, and Aunt Eliza is preparing to come here. But I do not see anyone preparing to go there. Why don't they try to get ready?"

A certain gentleman in the South before the Civil War had a pious slave, and when the master died, they told him he had gone to heaven. The old slave shook his head, "I'm afraid he's not gone there," he said. "But why, Ben?" he was asked. "Cause when he went north, or went on a journey to the Springs, he talked about it a long time, and got ready. I never heard him talk about going to heaven; never saw him get ready to go there!"

So there are a good many who don't get ready. Christ taught in the Sermon on the Mount:

> *Lay not up for yourselves treasures upon earth, where moth and rust doth corrupt, and where thieves break through and steal; but lay up for yourselves treasures in heaven, where neither moth nor rust doth corrupt, and where thieves do*

> *not break through nor steal: for where
> your treasure is, there will your heart
> be also.*   (Matthew 6:9–11)

Treasures of the Heart

It does not take a great while to tell
where a man's treasure is. In fifteen minutes
of conversation with most men, you can tell
whether their treasures are on earth or in
heaven. Talk to a statesman about the country, and you will see his eyes light up—you
will find he has his heart there. Talk to
some businessmen, and tell them where
they can make a thousand dollars, and see
their interest—their hearts are there. You
talk to fashionable people, who are living
just for fashion, of its affairs, and you will
see their eyes kindle—they are interested at
once; their hearts are there. Talk to a poli-
tician about politics, and you see how suddenly he becomes interested. But talk to a
child of God, who is laying up treasures in
heaven, about heaven and about his future
home, and see if there is any enthusiasm.
*"Where your treasure is, there will your heart
be also"* (verse 11).

Now, it is just as much a command for a man to lay up his treasures in heaven as it is that he should not steal. Some people think all the commandments are in those ten that were given back on Sinai. But, when Jesus Christ was here, He gave us a good many other commandments. There is another command- ment in this Sermon on the Mount, that we ought to *seek ye first the kingdom of God, and his righteouness; and all these things shall be added unto you*" (Matthew 6:33). There is a command that we are to lay up our treasures in heaven and not on earth. The reason there are so many broken hearts in this land—the reason there are so many disappointed people—is that they have been laying up their treasures down here.

The worthlessness of gold, for which so many are striving, is illustrated by a story that Dr. Arnott, the Scottish physician, used to tell. A ship carrying a company of emi- grants has been driven from her course and wrecked on a desert island, far from man's reach. There is no way of escape, but they have a good stock of food. The ocean sur- rounds them, but they have plenty of seeds, fine soil, and sunshine, so there is no danger. Before the plans are laid, an exploring party discovers a gold mine. The whole party goes to dig there. They labor day after day and month after month. They get large heaps of gold. But spring is past, and not a field has been cleared, not a grain of seed put into the ground. The summer comes and their wealth increases, but their stock of food grows small. In the fall, they find that their heaps of gold are worthless. Famine stares them in the face. They rush to the woods, chop down trees, dig up the roots, till the ground, and sow the seed. It is too late! Winter has come and their seeds rot in the ground. They die of want in the midst of their treasures.

The earth is like an island, and eternity is like the ocean around it. We have been cast on the island's shore. There is a living seed, but the gold mines attract us. We spend spring and summer there; winter overtakes us in our toil, and we are without the Bread of Life. We are lost. Let we who are Christians value even more the home that holds the treasures that no one can take away.

A Blackboard Lesson

Once when I was in San Francisco, I went into a Sunday school the first day I was there. It was a rainy day, and there were so few that the superintendent thought of dismissing them. But instead, he invited me to speak to the whole school as one class. The lesson was based on that passage from the Sermon on the Mount: *"Lay not up for yourselves treasures upon earth, where moth and rust doth corrupt, and where thieves break through and steal"* (Matthew 6:9). I invited a young man to the blackboard, and we proceeded to compare things that some people have on earth, and things that other people have in heaven.

"Now," said I, "name some earthly treasure."

They all shouted, "Gold."

"Well," I said, "I suppose that is your greatest treasure out here in California. What is another?"

A boy shouted, "Land."

"Well," I said, "we will put down land."

114

"What else do the people out here in California think a good deal of and have their hearts set on?"

They said, "Houses."

"Put that down. What else?"

"Pleasure."

"Put that down."

"Honor—fame."

"Put them down."

"Business."

"Yes," I said, "a great many people have got their hearts buried in their business—put that down." And, as if a little afraid, one of them said "Clothes," and the whole school smiled. "Put that down," I said. "Why, I believe there are some people in the world who think more of clothes than any other thing. They just live for their outward appearance."

Not long ago, I heard about a young lady who was dying of consumption. She had been living in the world and for the world, and it seemed as if the world had taken full possession of her. She thought she would die Thursday night, and so on Thursday she wanted them to crimp her hair so that she would look beautiful in her coffin. But she didn't die Thursday night. She lingered through Friday, and Friday she didn't want them to take her hair down. And her friends said that she looked very beautiful in the coffin! Just what people wear—the idea of people having their heart set on things of that kind!

"And what else, now?"

Well, they were a little ashamed to say it, but one said, "Rum."

"Well," I said, "put it down. There are many men who think more of the rum bottle than they do of the kingdom of God. They will give up their wives, their homes and mothers, character, and reputation forever for the rum bottle. Many men cry out, 'Give me rum, and I will give you heaven, and all its glories. I will sell my wife and children. I will make them beggars and paupers. I will degrade and disgrace them for the rum bottle. That is my treasure.' 'Oh, rum bottle!

I worship you,' is the cry of many—they turn their backs on heaven with all its glories for rum." Some of them thought, when that little boy said, "Rum," that he made a mistake, that it was not a treasure, but it is a treasure to thousands.

And after we finished, and thought of everything we could, I said, "Suppose we just write down some of the heavenly treasures. What is there that the Lord wants us to set our hearts and affections on?" They all said, "Jesus."

"That is good. We will put Him down first at the head of the list. Now what else?"

And, they said, "Angels."

"Put them down. We will have their society when we get to heaven. That is a treasure up there, truly. What else?"

"Well, the friends that have died in Christ, that have fallen asleep in Christ."

"Put them down. Death has taken them from us now, but we will be with them eventually. What else?"

"Crowns."

"Yes, we are going to have a crown, a crown of glory, a crown of righteousness, a crown that does not fade away. What else?"

"The tree of life."

"Yes," I said, "the tree of life. We will have a right to it. We can go to that tree and pluck its fruit, eat, and live forever. What else?"

"The river of life."

"Yes, we will walk on the banks of that clean river."

"Harps," another one said.

Another one said, "Palms."

"Yes," I said, "put them down. Those are treasures that we will have there."

"Purity."

"Yes, only the pure will be there. White robes, without spot or wrinkle on our garments. A great many find flaws in our characters down here, but Christ will present us before the Father without a spot or a wrinkle. We will stand there complete in Him," I said. "Can you think of anything else?"

One of them said, "Yes, we will have a new song. It is the song of Moses and the Lamb."

I don't know just who wrote it or how, but it will be a glorious song. I suppose the singing we have here on earth is nothing compared to the songs of that upper world. The principal thing we are told we are going to do in heaven is sing, and that is why men ought to sing down here. We ought to begin to sing here so that it won't seem strange when we get to heaven. I pity the professed Christian who does not have a song in his heart—who never feels like singing. It seems to me if we are truly children of God, we will want to sing about it. And so, when we get there, we can't help shouting out the loud hallelujahs of heaven.

Then I said, "Is there anything else?" Well, we continued until we had two columns of heavenly treasures. We stood there for a while and drew the contrast between the earthly and the heavenly treasures. When we decided to put them all down right beside Christ, the earthly treasures looked pretty small after all. What is a world full of gold compared to Jesus Christ? You who have Christ, would you like to part with

Him for gold? Would you like to give Him up for all the honor the earth can bestow on you for a few months or a few years? Think of Christ! Think of the treasures of heaven. And then think of these earthly treasures that we have out hearts set on, and that so many of us are living for.

God blessed that lesson on the blackboard in a marvelous way—the man who had been writing down the treasures on the board happened to be an unconverted Sunday school teacher. He had gone out there to California to make money, and his heart was set on gold. He was living for that instead of God.

That was the idol of his heart, but God convicted him at that blackboard. The first convert that God gave me on the Pacific coast was that man, and he was the last man that shook hands with me when I left San Francisco. He saw how empty the earthly treasures were, and how grand and glorious the riches of heaven were. Oh, if God would open your eyes—and I think if you are honest and ask Him to do it, He will—He will show you how empty this world is in comparison with what He has in store.

There are a great many people who wonder why they don't mount up on wings, as it were, and make some progress in the divine life. They wonder why they don't grow more in grace. I think the reason is that they have too many earthly treasures. We do not need to be rich to have our hearts set on riches.

We do not need to be in the world more than other people to have our hearts there. I believe the Prodigal was in the far country long before his feet got there. When his heart got there, he was there. And there are many men who do not mingle in the world as much as others do, but their hearts are there. They would be if they could, and God looks at the heart. Now, what we want to do is to obey the voice of the Master. Instead of laying up treasures on earth, lay them up in heaven. If we do that, bear in mind, we will never be disappointed.

It is clear that idolators are not going to enter the kingdom of God. I may make an idol of my business; I may make an idol of my wife; I may make idols of my children. I don't think you have to go to less civilized countries to find men guilty of idolatry. I think you will find many right here who have idols in their hearts. Let us pray that the Spirit of God may banish those idols from our hearts, that we may not be guilty of idolatry. Pray that we may worship God in spirit and in truth. Anything that comes between me and God is an idol—anything. I don't care what it is. Business is all right in its place, and there is no danger of my loving my family too much if I love God more. But, God must have the first place, and if He does not, then the idol is set up.

All Eternity for Rest

One of the great riches of heaven will be the possession of those desires of the soul, which are so often sought after down here but are never completely found—such as infinite knowledge, perfect peace, and satisfying love. Like a beautiful painting that has been marred—smeared all over with streaks of black, and then restored to its original beauty—so the soul is restored to its full beauty of color when it is washed with the blood of Jesus Christ. The senseless image on the canvas cannot be compared, in any way, to the living, rational soul.

If we could only see some of our friends who have gone on before us, we would probably feel like falling down before them. John—although he had seen so many strange things—fell to worship one of the bright angels who stood before him to reveal some of the secrets of heaven. He said:

> *And I John saw these things, and heard them. And when I had heard and seen, I fell down to worship before the feet of the angel which shewed me these things. Then saith he unto me, See thou do it not: lot I am thy fellow servant, and of thy brethren the prophets, and of them which keep the saying of this book: worship God.*
>
> (Revelation 22:8–9)

The diamond not only reflects the light, but is a little sun shining by a light of its own.

So the polished diamond of the soul reflects the beauty and light of God, and preserves its own personality as well.

The thirst for knowledge is one of our earthly desires. As much as sin has weakened man's mental faculties, it has not taken away his desire for knowledge. But with all his efforts, with all that he thinks he knows about astronomy, chemistry, geology, and the rest of the sciences, his knowledge of the secrets of nature is still limited. There are so many things we don't know. Thousands of astronomers have lived and died, the ages of the world have rolled on, and they found out that the planet Mars had two moons. Perhaps in ages to come someone will find out that they are not moons at all. This is what most of our human knowledge amounts to.

Not one of our college professors—and many of them have gone nearly everywhere the mind can reach—is not anxious to learn more and more, to find out new things, to make new discoveries. If we were as familiar with all the stars in the sky as we are with our own earth, we would still not be satisfied. Not until we are like God can we comprehend the infinite.

The imperfect glimpses of God that we get by faith only intensify our desire for more. For now, as Paul said, *"We see through a glass, darkly; but then face-to-face: now I know in part; but then shall I know even as also I am known"* (1 Corinthians 13:12). The word Paul used, properly translated, is "mirror." Now we see God in a looking glass—but then face-to-face.

Suppose we knew nothing of the sun except what we saw of its light reflected from the moon. Would we not wonder about its immense distance, its dazzling splendor, and its life-giving power? Now all that we see—the sun, the moon, the stars, the ocean, the earth, the flowers, and, above all, man— are a grand mirror in which the perfection of God is imperfectly reflected.

Another need that we have is rest. We get tired of working. Yet there is no real rest on earth.

There remaineth therefore a rest to the people of God. For he that is entered into his rest, he also hath ceased from his own works, as God did from his. Let us labour therefore to enter into that rest, lest any man fall after the same example of unbelief. (Hebrews 4:9–11)

Now, while we all want rest, I think a great many people make a mistake when they think the church is a place of rest. When they join the church, they have a false idea about their position in it. There are many who come in to rest. It says here that there remains a rest for the people of God, but it does not tell us that the church is a place of rest. We have all eternity to rest in. We are to rest by and by, but we are to work here on earth. When our work is finished, the Lord will call us home to enjoy that rest. There is no use in talking about rest down here in the enemy's country. We cannot rest in this world, where God's Son has been crucified and cast out. I think that many people are going to lose their reward just because they have come into the church with the idea that they are to rest there—as if the church was working for the reward, instead of each one building himself all over again, each one using all his influence toward the building of Christ's kingdom.

> *And I heard a voice from heaven saying unto me, Write, Blessed are the dead which die in the Lord from henceforth: Yea, saith the Spirit, that they may rest from their labours; and their works do follow them.* (Revelation 14:13)

Now, death may rob us of money. Death may rob us of position. Death may rob us of our friends. But, there is one thing death can never do, and that is rob us of the work that we do for God. That will live on forever. "Their works will follow them." How much are we doing? Anything that we do outside of ourselves, and not with a mean and selfish motive, *that* is going to live. We have the privilege of setting in motion streams of activity that will flow on even when we are dead and gone.

It is the privilege of everyone to live more in the future than they do in the present, so that their lives will mean more in fifty or a hundred years than they do now. John Wesley's influence is a thousand times greater today than it was when he was living. He still lives. He lives in the lives of thousands and hundreds of thousands of his followers. Martin Luther lives more today than he did centuries ago, when he was living in Germany. He only lived one life for a while. But now, look at the hundreds and thousands and millions of lives that he is living. There are between fifty and sixty million people who profess to be followers of the Lord Jesus Christ, as taught by Martin Luther. He is dead in the sight of the world, but his "works do follow him." He still lives.

The words of John the Baptist are ringing through the world today, although nearly 2,000 years have passed since he spoke them. Herod thought when he beheaded him that he was hushing his voice, but it is ringing all through the earth even today. John the Baptist lives because he lived for God. But, he has entered into his rest, and "his works do follow him." If they can see what is going on upon the earth, how much joy they must have in heaven to think that they have set these streams in motion, and that this work is going on—being carried on after them.

If a man lives a mean, selfish life, he goes down in the grave, and his name and everything goes down with him. If he is ambitious enough to leave a record behind him, with a selfish motive, his name rots with his body. But, if a man gets outside of himself and begins to work for God, his name will live forever. You may go to Scotland today, and you will find the influence of John Knox, the Scottish reformer, writer, and statesman, everywhere. It seems as if you could almost feel the breath of that man's prayer in Scotland today. His influence still lives. *"Blessed are the dead which die in the Lord...they may rest from their labours; and their works do follow them"* (Revelation 14:13). Blessed rest is in store for us. We will rest by and by, but we don't want to talk about rest down here.

If I am to wipe a tear from the cheek of that fatherless child, I must do it down here. Scripture does not say that we will have the privilege of doing that hereafter. If I am going to help some fallen man who has been overtaken by sin, I must do it here. Nowhere does Scripture teach that we are going to have the glorious privilege of working for

God in the world to come. We are not going to have the privilege of being coworkers with God in the future—but that is our privilege today. We may not have it tomorrow. It may be taken from us tomorrow, but we can enter into the vineyard and do something today before the sun goes down. We can do something now before we go to glory.

Another need that we feel down here is love. Heaven is the only place where the conditions of love can be fulfilled. There, it is essentially mutual. Everybody loves everybody else. In this world of wickedness and sin, it seems impossible for people to be perfectly equal. When we meet people who are bright, beautiful, and good, we have no difficulty in loving them. All the people of heaven will be like that. There will be no fear of misplaced confidences there. We will never be deceived by those we love. When a suspicion of doubt arises in anyone who loves, their happiness from that moment is at an end. There will be no suspicion in heaven.

Chapter 6

HEAVEN...ITS REWARDS

I shall be satisfied, The soul's vague longings,
The aching void which nothing earthly fills.
Oh! what desires upon my soul are thronging
As I look upward to the heavenly hills.

Thither my weak and weary steps are tending,
Savior and Lord! with thy frail child abide,
Guide me toward home, where all my wanderings ended,
I then shall see *Thee*, and *"be satisfied."*

HEAVEN...ITS REWARDS

If I understand things correctly, when you find a man or woman who is looking to be rewarded here for doing right, they are unqualified to work for God. Because, if they are looking for the applause of men—looking for the reward in this life—it will disqualify them for the service of God—they are continually compromising truth.

They are afraid of hurting someone's feelings. They are afraid that someone is going to say something against them, or write something against them. Now, we must trample the world under our feet if we are going to get our reward hereafter. If we live for God, we must suffer persecution. The kingdom of darkness and the kingdom of light are at war, and have been, and will be as long as Satan is permitted to reign in this world. As long as the kingdom of darkness is permitted to exist, there will be a conflict. If you want to be popular in the kingdom of God—if you want to be popular in heaven—and get a reward that will last forever, you will have to be unpopular here.

If you seek the applause of men, you can't have the Lord say, "Well done" at the end of the journey. You can't have both. Why? Because this world is at war with God. The idea that the world is getting better all the time is not true. The old, natural heart is just as much at odds with God as it was when Cain slew Abel. Sin leaped into the world full-grown in Cain. And from the time that Cain was born into the world to the present, man by nature has been at war with God. This world was not established in grace, and we have to fight the world, the flesh, and the devil. If we fight the world, the world won't like us. If we fight the flesh, the flesh won't like us. We have to mortify the flesh. We have to crucify the old man and put him under—then we will get our reward, and it will be a glorious one! It says in Luke 16:15:

> *And he said unto them, Ye are they which justify yourselves before men; but God knoweth your hearts: for that which is highly esteemed among men is abomination in the sight of God.*

We must go against the current of this world. If the world has nothing to say *against* us, we can be pretty sure that the Lord Jesus Christ has very little to say *for* us. There are those who do not like to go against the current of the world. They say they know this or that is wrong, but they do not say a word against it, fearing that it might make them unpopular. If we expect to receive the heavenly reward, we must fight the good fight of faith. For all such, as Paul has said, there is laid up a crown of righteousness, which the Lord the righteous judge will give us at that day (2 Timothy 4:8).

Fear of Death

How little we realize the meaning of the word *eternity*! The whole time between the creation of the world and the ending of it would not make a day in eternity. In time, it is like the infinity of space whose center is everywhere and whose boundary is nowhere. We read:

> *Forasmuch, then, as the children are partakers of flesh and blood, he also himself likewise took part of the same;*

134

that through death he might destroy him that had the power of death, that is the devil; and deliver them who through fear of death were all their lifetime subject to bondage. (Hebrews 2:14–15)

A great many of God's professed children live in constant bondage—in constant fear of death. I believe that it is dishonoring to God. I believe that it is not His will to have one of His children live in fear for one moment. If you know the truth as it is in Christ, you need not fear. If you know Christ, you do not need to worry, because death will only hasten you on to glory—and your name is already there.

And then, the next thought is for those who are dear to us. I believe that it is not only our privilege to have our names written in heaven, but also those of the children whom God has given us. Our hearts should go right out to them. The promise is not only to us, but to our children. Many a father's and many a mother's heart is burdened with anxiety for the salvation of their children. If your own name is there, let your next aim in life be to get the children that God has given you there, also.

I have three children, and the greatest desire of my heart is that they may be saved—that I may know that their names are written in the Book of Life. I may be taken from them early. I may leave them in this changing world without a father's care, without a father to watch over them. And, I have often said to myself, I would rather have them come to my grave after I am dead and gone, drop a tear on it, and say, "My father cared for my soul," than do anything else.

A mother died in one of our eastern cities a few years ago, and she had a large family of children. She had tuberculosis, and the children were brought in to her when she was dying. When the oldest one was brought in, she gave her last message and her dying blessing. And, when the next one was brought in, she put her hand on the child's head and gave her blessing. And then, the next one was brought in, and the next, until at last they brought in the little infant. She took it to her bosom and pressed it to her loving heart. Her friends saw that it was hastening her end, that she was excited. As they went to take the little child from her, she said, "My husband, I charge you to bring all these children home with you." And so, God charges us as parents to bring our children home with us. He commands us to not only have our own names written in heaven, but those of our children, also.

An eminent Christian worker in New York told me a story that affected me very much. A father had a son who had been sick some time, but he did not consider him in danger. Until one day, he came home to dinner and found his wife weeping, and he asked, "What is the matter?"

"There has been a great change in our boy since this morning," the mother said, "and I am afraid that he is dying. I wish you would go in and see him. If you think he is dying, I wish you would tell him so. I cannot bear to tell him."

The father went in, sat down by the bedside, and placed his hand on his son's forehead. He could feel the cold, damp sweat of death, and knew its cold, icy hand was feeling for the cords of life. He knew that his boy was soon to be taken away, and he said to him, "My son, do you know you are dying?"

The little fellow looked up at him and said, "No, am I? Is this death that I feel stealing over me, Father?"

"Yes, my son, you are dying."

"Will I live the day out?"

"No, you may die at any moment."

He looked up to his father and said, "Well, I will be with Jesus tonight, won't I, Father?"

And the father answered, "Yes, my boy, you will spend tonight with the Savior." The father turned away to conceal the tears, so that the little boy would not see him weep.

But, the child saw the tears, and he said, "Father, don't you weep for me. When I get to heaven I will go straight to Jesus and tell Him that ever since I can remember you have tried to lead me to Him."

I would rather have my children say that about me after I am dead and gone—or if they die before me I would rather they took that message to the Master—than to have a monument over me reaching to the skies. We should not look on death as we do. The English bishop of Calcutta, Reginald Hebei, has written of a dead friend:

Thou art gone to the grave, but we will not deplore thee,
Though sorrow and darkness encompass the tomb;
Thy Savior has passed through its portals before thee,
And the lamp of His love is thy guide through the gloom;
Thou art gone to the grave, we no longer behold thee,
Nor tread the tough paths of the world by thy side,
But the wide arms of Mercy are spread to enfold thee,
And sinners may die, since the Sinless has died.

The roll is being called, and one after another are being summoned away. But if their names are there, if we know that they are there, saved, how sweet it is, after they have left us, to think that we will meet them eventually. How wonderful it is to think that we will see them in the morning when the night has passed into day.

During the last war, a young man lay on a cot, and they heard him say, "Here, here!" Someone went to his cot and wanted to know what he wanted, and he said, "Hark! Hush! Don't you hear them?"

"Hear who?" was asked.

"They are calling the roll of heaven," he said, and pretty soon he answered, "Here!"— and he was gone. If our names are in the Book of Life, our name is called, we can say with Samuel, "Here, Lord Jesus," and fly away to meet Him. And if our children are called away early, it is so sweet to think that they die in Christ. How comforting to know that the great Shepherd gathers them in His arms, carries them in His bosom, and that we will meet them once again.

Paul, the Christian Hero

The way to get to heaven is to be saved through faith in Jesus Christ. Salvation is a gift, but we have to work it out, just as if we had received a gold mine for a gift. I don't get a crown by joining church or renting a pew.

There was Paul. He got his crown. He had many hard fights; he met Satan on a good many battlefields, and he overcame him and wore the crown. It would take about ten thousand average Christians of this day to make one Paul. When I read the life of that apostle, I blush for the Christianity of this century. It is a weak and sickly thing.

See what Paul went through. He was severely beaten five times. The old Roman custom of beating was to take the prisoner and bind his wrists together, bend him over in a stooping posture, and, with sharp pieces of steel braided into a lash, the Roman soldier would bring the lash down on the bare back of the prisoner. It would cut him through the skin, so that men sometimes died in the very act of being beaten. But, Paul said he was beaten five different times. Now, if we should get one stripe on our backs, what whining there would be. There would be forty publishers after us before the sun went down, and they would want to publish our lives, so that they could make money on it. But Paul says, *"Five times received I forty stripes save one"* (2 Corinthians 11:24). That was nothing for him. Take your stand by his side.

"Paul, you have been beaten by these Jews four times, and they are going to give you thirty-nine more stripes. What are you going to do after you get out of the difficulty? What are you going to do about it all?"

"Do?" said he, "I will do this one thing: I press toward the mark for the prize of my high calling. I am on my way to get my crown" (Philippians 3:13–14). He was not going to lose his crown. "Don't think that a few stripes will turn me away; these light afflictions are nothing." And so they put on thirty-nine more stripes.

He had sprung into the race for Christ, and was leaping toward heaven. If you will allow me the expression, the devil met his match when he came against Paul. He never got sidetracked. He never sat down to write a letter to defend himself. All the strength that he had, he gave to Christ. He never gave a care to the world nor to defending himself. One thing I do, he said, I am not going to lose the crown. See that no man takes your crown. He was beaten with rods three times. Take your stand beside him again.

"Now, Paul, they have beaten you twice, and they are going to beat you again. What are you going to do? Are you going to continue preaching? It you are, let me give you a little advice. Now, don't be quite so radical—be a little more conservative. Just use a little finer language, and kind of cover up the cross with beautiful words and flowery sentences. Tell men that they are pretty good after all—that they are not so bad. And, try to pacify the Jews; make friends with them. Get in with the world, and the world will think more of you. Don't be so earnest; don't be so radical, Paul. Now come, take our advice. What are you going to do?"

"Do?" he said, "This one thing I do—I press toward the mark of the prize of my high calling." So they hit him with the rods, and every blow lifted him nearer to God. Take your stand again. They began to stone him. That is the way they killed those who did not preach to suit them. It seemed as if he was about to be paid back in his own coin, for when Stephen was stoned to death, Paul, then known as Saul, cheered on the crowd.

"Now, Paul, this is growing serious. Hadn't you better take back some of the things you have said about Christ? What are you going to do?"

"Do?" he said, "if they take my life, I will only get the crown sooner." He would not budge an inch. He had something that the world could not give. He had something it could not take away. He had eternal life, and he had a crown of glory in store for him.

These Light Afflictions

Three times he was shipwrecked—a day and a night in the deep. Look at that mighty apostle; he was stranded in the ocean a whole day and night. There he was—shipwrecked, and for what? Was it to make money? He was not after money. He was just going from city to city, and town to town, to preach the glorious gospel of Jesus Christ. He only wanted to lift up the cross wherever he had the opportunity. He went down to Corinth and preached eighteen months. And, he didn't have a lot of the leading ministers of Corinth to come on the platform and sit by his side when he preached. Not a single man stood by him.

When he got down to Corinth, he didn't have some of the leading businessmen to stand by him and advise him. The little tent-maker arrived in Corinth a perfect stranger and the first thing he did was find a place where he could make a tent. He did not go to a hotel; his means would not allow it. But, he went where he could make his bread by the sweat of his brow. Think of that great apostle making a tent, and then getting on the corner of a street and preaching. Perhaps once in awhile he would get into a synagogue, but the Jews would turn him out. They didn't want to hear him preach anything about Jesus the crucified. The Jews didn't like that; they turned him out, and, after he toiled eighteen months, they took him outside of the city and gave him thirty-nine stripes, and paid him off. That was all the pay he got, and they sent him onto the next town.

When I read about the life of such a man, I am ashamed to think how sickly and dwarfed Christianity is at the present time. There are many hundreds who never think of working for the Son of God and honoring Christ.

Yet, when Paul wrote that letter back to Corinth, we find him taking inventory of some things he had. He was rich, he said,

In journeyings often, in perils of waters, in perils of robbers, in perils by my own countrymen, in perils by the heathen, in perils in the city, in perils in the wilderness, in perils in the sea, in perils among false brethren. (2 Corinthians 11:26)

That last must have been the hardest of all.

In weariness and painfulness, in watchings often, in hunger and thirst, in fastings often, in cold and in nakedness. Beside those things...the care of all the churches. (2 Corinthians 11:27–28)

These are only some of the things that he summed up. Do you know what made him so exceedingly glad? It was because he believed Scripture—he believed the Sermon on the Mount. We profess to believe it. We pretend to believe it. But, few of us more than half believe it. Listen to one sentence in that sermon: *"Rejoice, and be exceeding glad: for great is your reward in heaven when you are persecuted*" (Matthew 5:12). Now this perse-cution was about all that Paul had.

That was his capital, and he had a good deal of it. He had endured a good many per-secutions, and he was to get a great reward. Christ says: Rejoice and be exceeding glad, for great is your reward. If Jesus Christ called it great, it must be wonderful. We call things great that may look very small to Jesus Christ. Things that look very small to us may look very large to Christ. When the great Christ, the Creator of heaven and earth—He who created the heavens and the earth by His mighty power—calls it a great reward, it must be so.

Perhaps some people said to him, "Now, Paul, you are meeting with too much opposi-tion. You are suffering too much."

Hear him reply: "*For our light affliction, which is but for a moment, worketh for us a far more exceeding and eternal weight of glory*" (2 Corinthians 4:17).

"These light afflictions," he called them. We would call them pretty hard, pretty heavy, wouldn't we? But he said, in effect,

"These light afflictions are nothing. Think of the glory before me, and think of the crowning time. Think of the reward that is laid up for me. I am on my way. He will give it to me when the time comes." That is what filled his soul with joy—it was the reward that the Lord had in store for him.

Now, my friends, let us just for a minute think about what he accomplished. Think of going out among the heathen. Think of being the first missionary to preach to these men—who were so full of wickedness, hatred, and bitterness—the glorious gospel of Jesus Christ. Think of telling them that the man who died the death of a common prisoner—a common felon—in the sight of the world, outside the walls of the city of Jerusalem, was the Christ. Think of telling them that they had to believe in that crucified man in order to get into the kingdom of God.

Think of the dark mountain that rose up before Paul. Think of the opposition, the bitter persecution. And then think of the insignificant obstacles in our way. But a great many worldly people think Paul's life was a failure. Probably his enemies thought that putting him in prison would silence him. But, I believe today Paul thanks God more for prisons, for stripes, for persecution, and for the opposition that he suffered, than for anything else that happened to him here. The very things we don't like are sometimes the very best for us.

Christians would probably not have these glorious epistles if Paul had not been thrown into prison. There he took up his pen and began to write that letter to the Christians at Corinth. Look at the two epistles that he wrote to the Corinthians. Look and see how much has been done for the world by these epistles. See what a blessing they have been to the church of God—how they have thrown light on many lives. But we might not have those epistles if it had not been for opposition.

No doubt John Bunyan blesses God more today for Bedford jail than anything that happened to him. Probably we would not have *The Pilgrim's Progress* if he had not been thrown into that jail. Satan thought he accomplished a great deal when he shut Bunyan up twelve years and six months in that jail. But, what a blessing it was to the world. And, I believe Paul blesses God today for the Philippian jail, and for the opposition he encountered in Rome, because it gave him time to write those blessed letters. Think of Alexander making the world tremble with the tread of his armies, and of Caesar and Napoleon's power. But, here is a little tent-maker who, without any army, moved the world. Why? Because God Almighty was with him.

He said in one place, "*None of these things move me*" (Acts 20:24). They threw him in prison, but it was all the same—it did not move him. When he was at Corinth and Athens preaching, it was all the same. He just pressed toward the mark of the prize of his high calling. If God wanted him to go through prisons to win the prize, it was all the same to him. They put him in prison, but they put the Almighty in with him. He was so linked to Jesus that they could not separate them. He would rather be in prison with Christ than out of prison without Him. A thousand times over, he would rather be cast into prison with the Son of God and suffer a little persecution for a few days here, than to be living without Him.

He went over into Macedonia. He heard the cry, "Come over into Macedonia, and help us." He went over, he preached, and the first thing that happened to him was that he was put into the Philippian jail. Now, if he had been as fainthearted as most of us, he would have been disappointed and cast down. There would have been a good deal of complaint. He would have said, "This is a strange thing to have happened. What ever brought me here? I thought the Lord called me here, yet, here I am in prison in a strange city. How did I ever get here? How will I ever get out of this place? I have no money. I have no friends. I have no attorney. I have no one to intercede for me, and here I am."

Paul and Silas were not only in prison, but their feet were also held firmly in the stocks There they were, in the inner prison, the inner dungeon, a dark, cold, damp dungeon. But at midnight, those prisoners heard a strange voice. They had never heard anything like it before. They heard singing. I don't know what song they sang, but I know one thing—it was not a doleful sound from the tombs. You know we have a hymn, "Hark, from the tombs a doleful sound." They didn't sing that, but the Bible tells us they sang praises. That was an odd place to sing praises, wasn't it?

I suppose it was time for the evening prayers, that they had just had them, and then sang their evening song. God answered their prayers, and the old prison shook, the chains fell off, and the prison doors were opened. Yes—yes—I have no doubt he thanks God in glory that he went to jail and that the Philippian jailer became converted.

Swept into Glory

But look at Paul in Rome. Nero has signed his death warrant. Take your stand and look at the little man. He is small. In the sight of the world, he is contemptible—the world frowns on him. Go to the palace of the king and talk about that criminal—about Paul—and you will see a sneer on their faces. "Oh, he is a fanatic," they say. "He has gone mad." I wish the world was filled with such lunatics. I tell you, what we need today are a few lunatics like him—men who fear nothing but sin and love no one but God.

Rome never had such a conqueror within its limits. Rome never had such a mighty man as Paul within its boundaries. Although the world looked down on him, and he looked very small and contemptible, yet in the sight of heaven he was the mightiest man that ever walked the streets of Rome. There will probably never be another one like him to travel those streets. The Son of God walked with him. There he is in that prison, and they come to him to tell him that Nero has signed his death warrant. He does not tremble; he is not afraid.

"Paul, are you not sorry you have been so zealous for Christ? It is going to cost you your life. If you had to live your live over again, would you give it to Jesus of Nazareth?" What do you think the old warrior would say?

See that eye light up as he says, "If I had ten thousand lives, I should give every one to Christ, and the only regret I have is that I did not commence earlier and serve Him better. The only regret I have now is that I ever lifted my voice against Jesus of Nazareth."

"But they are going to behead you."

"Well, they may take my head, but the Lord has my heart. I don't care about my head. The Lord has my heart. The Lord has my heart and has had it for years. They cannot separate me from the Lord, and though my head may be taken off, we are not going to be separated." (See Romans 8:39.) And they led him out.

I don't know; perhaps it was early in the morning. Secular history tells us that they led him two miles out of the city. Look at the little tentmaker as he goes through the streets of Rome with a firm pace. Look at that giant as he moves through the streets. He is on his way to the execution. Take your stand by his side and hear him talk. He is talking of the glory beyond. He says,

"Henceforth there is laid up for me a crown of righteousness. I shall be there tonight, I shall see the King in His beauty tonight, I have longed to be with Him. I have longed to see Him. This is my crowning day." (See 2 Timothy 4:8.)

The world pitied him, but he did not need its pity. He had something the world did not have. He had a love and zeal burning within him which the world knew nothing about. Ah, the love that Paul had for Jesus Christ! But the hour has come. The way they used to behead men in those days was for the prisoner to bend his head; a Roman soldier would take a sharp sword and cut it off. The hour had come, and, with a joyful countenance, I can see Paul bending that blessed head of his, and that sword coming down to set his spirit free.

If our eyes could look as Elisha's looked, we would have seen him leap into a chariot of light like Elijah. We would have seen him go sweeping through limitless space. Look at him now as he mounts higher and higher. Look at him, see him move up, up, up, ever upward. Look at him yonder! See! He is now entering the Eternal City of the glorified saints—the blissful abode of the Savior's redeemed. The prize he has sought for so long is at hand. See yonder the gates, how they fly wide open. See the herald angels yonder on the shining battlements of heaven. Hear the glad shouts that are passed along, "He is coming! He is coming!" And he goes sweeping through the pearly gates, up through the shining way, to the very throne of God, and Christ stands there and says, *"Well done, thou good and faithful servant...enter thou into the joy of thy lord"* (Matthew 25:21).

Just think of hearing the Master say that—that is enough for everything, is it not? Oh, friends, your turn and mine will come eventually, if we are faithful. Let us make sure that we do not lose the crown. Let us awake and put on the whole armor of God. Let us press into the conflict; it is a glorious privilege. And then to us, too—as to the glorified of old—that blessed welcome, "Well done, thou good and faithful servant," will come.

About the Author

DWIGHT LYMAN MOODY
(1837–1899)

On February 5, 1837, in Northfield, Massachusetts, Dwight Lyman Moody was born, the sixth in what would be a family of nine children. His father died when Moody was only a tender child, leaving little provision for the family. Hence, Moody learned the value of hard work at an early age. An ambitious Moody went to Boston at the age of seventeen, where he became a successful salesman in his uncle's shoe store. His uncle made him promise to go to church, a promise that he faithfully kept, and he was won to the Lord by his Sunday school teacher.

In 1856 Moody went to Chicago, where he continued to succeed as a shoe salesman. His fervor in selling shoes was exceeded, however, by his zeal in winning souls, and he began to pack the pews of the church with young men. At the age of twenty-three he devoted himself to full-time Christian work. Because of his poor grammar, his first attempts at public speaking were not well received by all: one deacon told him that he would serve God best by keeping still. Nonetheless, Moody persevered, and he became famous nationwide for his Sunday school work. He was also known for his ministry to the soldiers during the Civil War; many were brought to Christ through his meetings and through his distribution of Bibles and tracts.

In 1867 Moody traveled to Great Britain to learn new methods in Christian work. It was there that his heart was stirred and forever changed by these words, spoken to him by a well-known evangelist: "The world has yet to see what God will do with...the man who is fully consecrated to Him." Moody determined to be that man.

The road of full commitment was not without trials. In 1871 the church that Moody pastored, the largest church in Chicago, was destroyed in the Chicago fire. But in the wake of this disaster, Moody received the filling of the Holy Spirit. Never before had he experienced such a mighty revelation of God's love. After this empowering of the Spirit, Moody went on to accomplish even more for Christ. He held meetings in America, England, and Scotland, where thousands were in attendance and many were brought to Christ, and founded Moody Bible Institute.

When Moody died in 1899, he left a rich legacy: three Christian schools, a Christian publishing business, and a million souls won for Christ. The day of his death was not a sad day; rather, Moody exclaimed, "This is my triumph; this is my coronation day!"

Smith Wigglesworth on Heaven
Smith Wigglesworth

Illustrating his insights with many dramatic, real-life examples, Smith Wigglesworth has a dynamic message in store for those who are looking toward the Second Coming. He explains how to prepare for your future in eternity with God while experiencing the power and joy of the Holy Spirit in the present. Discover God's plans for you in this life and what He has in store for you in heaven. You can know victorious living—now and for all eternity.

ISBN: 978-0-88368-954-7 • Trade • 224 pages

www.whitakerhouse.com